CW00369776

Roberta Longstaff, SRD, has worked as a nutritional adviser in industry and in hospitals, and as a tutor in nutrition. She was last appointed the post of Area Dietitian for the Oxfordshire Area Health Authority and was a member of the Executive Committee of the British Dietetic Association's Council. She remains a key member of Dr Mann's team and has written the recipes for two bestselling books in the Positive Health Guide series: *The Diabetics' Diet Book* and *The Diabetics' Cookbook*.

Roberta Longstaff has always been interested in preventive medicine and firmly believes that the whole population will benefit from a low-fat, high-fibre diet. She has lived for a number of years in North America and the Far East where she collected many of her recipes.

Jim Mann has recently moved to New Zealand to take up an appointment as Professor of Human Nutrition at the University of Otago, Dunedin.

Prior to this, Professor Jim Mann was Honorary Consultant Physician at the Radcliffe Infirmary and John Radcliffe Hospital in Oxford, and University Lecturer in Social and Community Medicine at Oxford University.

He has been involved in the treatment of hyperlipidaemic patients and research into the various aspects of hyperlipidaemia and the prevention of coronary heart disease for 18 years, and ran the Lipid Clinic in Oxford from 1973.

Professor Mann was a member of both NACNE and COMA and was also a member of JACNE (Joint Advisory Committee on Nutritional Education). In addtion to writing booklets for hyperlipidaemic patients and for doctors treating the disease, he is author of the bestselling *Diabetics' Diet Book* and co-author of its sequel, *The Diabetics' Cookbook*, both published by Optima, as well as numerous scientific papers and articles.

O P T I M A

(X) POSITIVE HEALTH GUIDE

THE HEALTHY HEART DIET BOOK

Enjoy delicious low-fat, high-fibre recipes

Roberta Longstaff, SRD
and
Professor Jim Mann

Foreword by Peter Sleight, MD, DM, FRCP
Professor of Cardiovascular Medicine,
John Radcliffe Hospital, Oxford

© Roberta Longstaff and Jim Mann 1986

First published in the United Kingdom in 1986 by
Martin Dunitz Limited, London
Reprinted 1986

This edition published in 1988 by
Macdonald Optima, a division of
Macdonald & Co. (Publishers) Ltd
Reprinted 1989.

A member of Maxwell Pergamon Publishing Corporation plc

All rights reserved

No part of this publication may be reproduced,
stored in a retrieval system, or transmitted,
in any form or by any means without the prior
permission in writing of the publisher, nor be
otherwise circulated in any form of binding or
cover other than that in which it is published
and without a similar condition including this
condition being imposed on the subsequent
purchaser.

British Library Cataloguing in Publication Data

Longstaff, Roberta
    The healthy heart diet book.
    1. Food : Low fat dishes — Recipes
    2. Food : High fibre dishes — Recipes
    I. Title   II. Mann, Jim   III. Series
    641.5'638

    ISBN 0-356-14488-7

Macdonald & Co. (Publishers) Ltd
66–73 Shoe Lane,
London EC4P 4AB.

Photoset in Garamond
Printed and bound in Singapore

A substantial proportion of the royalties from the sale of this book will be given to the Simon Broome Heart Research Trust, a charity supporting research into the prevention of heart disease. Further details about the work of this Trust may be obtained from: The Secretary to the Trustees, Simon Broome Heart Research Trust, 4 The Green, Brill, Nr Aylesbury, Bucks.

Front cover photograph shows: *Chicken casserole (left, see page 68); Pasta tubes with petits pois (top, see page 47); Strawberries in champagne (right, see page 82); Chicken and tarragon pâté with walnuts (bottom, see page 77)*

CONTENTS

Acknowledgements 7
Foreword 8
Introduction 9
Food tables 22
Cooking for a healthy heart 25

Soups and starters 31
Salads 36
Vegetable dishes 41
Rice and pasta 44
Pulses 50
Fish, poultry and meat 60
Entertaining 75
Desserts 88
Baking 93
Dressings and sauces 100
Snacks 103
Daily meal plans 112
Eating out 118
Packed snacks 119
Catering for buffet meals 120
Index 123

ACKNOWLEDGEMENTS

We would like to thank the following for their help in the preparation of this book: David Cunningham, FHCI, MRSH, for his work as catering consultant; Honor Scattergood (née Runciman), SRD, for market research; Susan Lousley, SRD, for computer analysis; Anne Reeve and Grace Seccombe for typing the manuscript; Mary Vun, SRD, and Jacqueline Edington, SRD, for their comments; Sally Jones, our editor.

Most of the food analysis figures are based on *McCance and Widdowson's The Composition of Foods* (4th rev ed) by A. A. Paul and D. A. T. Southgate; and *Food Composition Tables for Use in East Asia* by the Food and Agriculture Organization. Additional food analysis was supplied by Dr D. A. T. Southgate and Dr Anne Walker. Granose Foods Ltd supplied the soya bran analysis.

Roberta Longstaff and Jim Mann   *1986*

The publishers are grateful to the following for their help in the preparation of this book: Peter Myers, assisted by Neil Mersh, for the photography; Mike Rose for art direction; Penny Markham for styling; Lisa Collard for food preparation.

FOREWORD

Peter Sleight, MD, DM, FRCP, Professor of Cardiovascular Medicine, John Radcliffe Hospital, Oxford

British doctors have recently become much more impressed by the evidence linking coronary heart disease with food, particularly as modern food intake is high in animal fat and low in fish. In North America the dangers of such a diet have been more strongly emphasised and American eating habits have changed dramatically over the last ten to twenty years as a result of this publicity. The food and dairy industries have responded to consumer demand and polyunsaturated margarine and skimmed or modified milk are widely available. Coronary disease and coronary deaths have fallen dramatically over this period and at least part of this fall is likely to be due to better eating habits.

Changing to a healthier diet need not be a penance. This new book by our expert and long established team will help you enjoy the change to healthier eating. It is attractively illustrated and the recipes clear. They are used here in Oxford and are proven in practice. Some doctors argue that a change in diet is only necessary for the relatively few people who have very high levels of cholesterol in their blood. Other doctors argue that all of us in Western Society have abnormally high cholesterol levels and therefore we should all alter our eating habits.

I believe the latter approach is better. It has been shown to be practical in other countries and is beginning to be accepted more widely in Britain. This book will help to make the change to a healthier diet not only painless but positively enjoyable.

INTRODUCTION

Who will benefit from a low-fat, high-fibre diet?

The short answer to this question is that everyone will benefit from a change to a balanced low-fat, high-fibre diet, apart from those people who have already made the change. This book will describe how all the family can enjoy a healthy low-fat diet, with the minimum of effort. It will not entail large cut-backs and restrictive eating, but a varied and tasty diet that will be of benefit to all.

Various statistics from countries throughout the world show us the advantages of a low-fat, high-fibre diet. A high-fat diet is a major cause of coronary heart disease (CHD – see page 14). This disease can cause heart attacks and is one of the commonest causes of death and ill-health at all ages over 35 years. It is not only adults who should follow a low-fat, high-fibre diet to help make them less susceptible to heart attacks. Children (over 5 years of age) should also follow this diet so they will grow up to appreciate the importance of healthy eating and know about the risks.

Why make the change?

There are important health reasons for making the change to a

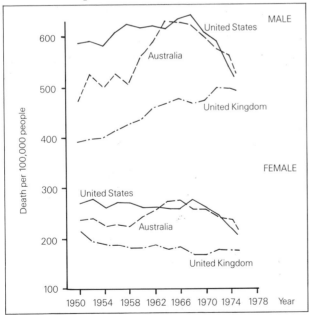

Deaths by coronary heart disease in UK, USA and Australia 1950–1975

low-fat diet. You may be encouraged to learn that in some countries, for example the United States of America and Australia, the number of deaths from coronary heart disease is decreasing (see diagram on page 9). It seems that a change in diet and eating habits in these countries, along the lines that will be suggested in this book, explains at least part of this beneficial trend. Among other countries where the diet has not changed significantly in recent years, for example Great Britain, heart attack rates remain steady. In fact, Scotland and Northern Ireland have amongst the highest rates in the world.

In some parts of the world, notably rural Africa and China, the inhabitants traditionally follow a low-fat, high-fibre diet and at the same time, have low rates of coronary heart disease, diabetes and some cancers. Conversely, in a few countries, for example Poland and Yugoslavia, the number of people dying from CHD has recently started to increase in parallel with a tendency to increase the amount of fat in their diet.

Official recommendations from national health departments in many affluent countries, for example the Department of Health COMA panel in the United Kingdom and the National Institutes of Health in the United States, have now suggested that the entire population will benefit from a general reduction in fat and an increase in fibre-rich carbohydrate. While this change is likely to be good for everyone, there is at least one group of people for whom this change is particularly necessary:

Those found to have raised levels of cholesterol (hypercholesterolaemia – see page 13) in the blood.

If you have been advised to change your diet because of hypercholesterolaemia, you can rest assured that the recommended eating pattern, as described in this book, is suitable for everyone in the family, even the children.

Do we need fat in the diet?

Some fat in our diet is essential for the following reasons:

- It is a useful and concentrated source of energy. Fat provides us with 9 kcal/g of energy, compared with 3.75 kcal/g from carbohydrates and 4 kcal/g from protein;
- It provides us with some essential vitamins, such as the fat soluble vitamins A, D and E, and fatty acids.

The important recommendation concerning fat is to eat less of it and to eat the right type of fat. Not all fats are equally bad for you and it is therefore necessary to distinguish between the different types.

What is fat and how is it used in the body?

Most people think of the fat we eat in terms of butter, margarine, oil, lard and the visible fat on meat. We often forget that there is a less obvious kind of fat, the so-called 'invisible' fat found in protein-rich foods such as milk, cheese and even red meat, between the muscle layers. Many processed foods contain a great deal of fat as well.

Most of the fats in our blood and body cells are similar in structure to the fat we eat. However, the fat in our diet must first be broken down into smaller units in the intestine, and then reconstructed after absorption.

If the fats are not immediately required for energy, they are stored in fat layers under the skin and around the body organs. These stores are easily reconverted into energy when needed.

There are two types of fat in the body:
Cholesterol is a fat-like, waxy material, present in the blood and most tissues in the body, especially nervous tissue. Cholesterol is an essential part of the body cell walls and an ingredient of many hormones and bile salts. When cholesterol is present in the blood stream in excessive amounts, it tends to build up in the walls of the arteries (see page 13).

Most of the body's cholesterol is made in the liver. Diet and hereditary influences determine the level of cholesterol in the blood.

Triglyceride is also found in the blood and is the form in which fat, not immediately required for energy, is stored around the body. Very high levels of triglycerides in the blood may be associated with an increase in heart attacks, but the relationship is not as clear as that established with blood cholesterol levels (see page 13).

Dietary fat: the main determinant of blood cholesterol

Certain foods are rich in cholesterol and, if eaten in very large amounts, they may increase blood cholesterol (examples of such foods are egg yolks, certain shellfish and offal). However, the main dietary determinant of blood cholesterol is the quantity and type of fat in our diet.

Saturated fats are generally solid at room temperature – common examples being butter and lard – and they usually originate from animal products, for example butter from milk, but some margarines can be made from saturated vegetable fats.

A diet rich in saturated fat has been shown to increase blood cholesterol, so consumption of this type of fat needs to be reduced as far as possible on a low-fat diet.

Polyunsaturated fats, on the other hand, are usually liquid or soft at room temperature – for example oils and soft margarines – and are extracted from plants, such as sunflowers and corn. They con-

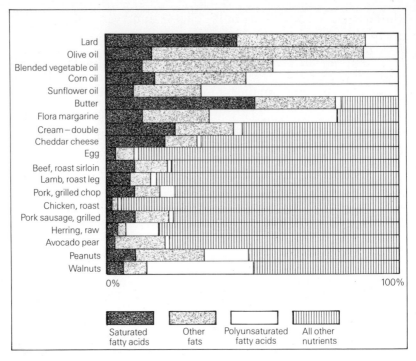

The composition of fats

tain some essential fatty acids needed to maintain good health.

Researchers have shown that polyunsaturated fats help to lower blood cholesterol so they should be used instead of saturated animal fat wherever possible. It is important to remember, however, that the overall aim of a low-fat diet is to keep total fat intake low. Polyunsaturated fats should not be used in excessive quantities themselves, as if to compensate for not using saturated fat, because we still need to reduce total fat consumption from the present average levels of 40 per cent of daily energy values to between 30 and 35 per cent.

Monounsaturated fats are also liquid at room temperature and the best known example is olive oil. This type of fat has no effect on blood cholesterol, that is, it neither increases nor decreases the level of cholesterol in the blood. So these fats can be included in a low-fat diet, in moderation.

The diagram above shows some of the commonest sources of different types of fat.

It may seem misleading that a low-fat diet will reduce cholesterol levels in the blood – Why not just a low-cholesterol diet? Saturated fat has the ability to raise cholesterol, and poly-unsaturated fats help to decrease it. The precise mechanism is unknown, but the effect of the type of fat on blood cholesterol is much greater than the effect of cholesterol in the diet.

There are no major recommendations about reducing choles-terol itself in the diet. In fact, the present tendency for people to buy cholesterol-free mixed cooking oils may well reflect a desire to eat a healthier diet, but they are being misled because many of the cholesterol-free oils are high in saturated fatty acids. It is much more important to use low-fat ingredients to make sure the saturated fat content is low.

Hereditary influences   In some families, there is a tendency for high blood cholesterol levels to be inherited. There are several conditions in which this tendency is passed down from parent to child – for example, in the condition known as familial hyper-cholesterolaemia (FH). If someone in your family is known to have FH, it is very important that all other members of the family ask their doctors to check their blood cholesterol level, to see if anyone else has the condition. A low-fat diet has been shown to play a very important part in the treatment of this disease because it helps to lower blood cholesterol.

Cholesterol and heart disease

As we have seen, the amount and type of fat in the diet is more important than the quantity of cholesterol we eat.

A diet high in saturated fat is associated with high levels of cholesterol in the blood; but a low intake of saturated fat and modest increase in polyunsaturated fat result in a lower blood cholesterol.

These are important facts because a high level of cholesterol in the blood is, in turn, associated with a tendency for cholesterol to be deposited in the walls of blood vessels. This is particularly serious when it affects the walls of the arteries supplying the heart muscle; they become narrower and may cause CHD. There is a clear relationship between the level of blood cholesterol and the risk of heart attacks.

There is, however, no clear or well-defined figure below which one can safely say that the cholesterol level is normal, but the risk does seem to be very low when blood cholesterol levels are below 5 mml/litre (190 mmol/100 ml). The risk of heart attacks steadily increases above this value. This figure is particularly relevant to people whose cholesterol levels are determined by hereditary influences.

High density lipoprotein (HDL)

This is a substance in the blood stream which may indirectly help

to prevent heart disease. It helps to get rid of unnecessary cholesterol, and prevents it from being deposited on the walls of arteries.
High levels are, therefore, helpful in reducing the risk of narrowing of the arteries and heart disease. HDL cannot be consumed in
the diet; it is made in the body. But the kind of diet which helps to
lower cholesterol – low saturated fat, modest polyunsaturated fat
– also helps to maintain adequate levels of HDL.

So, the overall message about fat in the diet is:
- Reduce all saturated fat as much as possible to help lower
  blood cholesterol;
- Use polyunsaturated (or monounsaturated) fats in moderation
  and when necessary, to keep blood cholesterol levels low;
- Keep total fat intake to a lower average level of 30–35 per
  cent of total daily energy intake.

The healthy heart

What is coronary heart disease and who is at risk?
Heart disease, heart attacks, angina, atherosclerosis and coronary
heart disease (CHD) are terms bandied about by people who often
do not realize what the words mean. In most countries, heart disease is an important cause of ill-health and early death. Many
people in Western countries regard heart disease as synonymous
with the other terms listed above. This is quite wrong because, as
heart disease is a general term covering all diseases of the heart,
there is obviously more than one type of disease. In developing
countries, rheumatic heart disease (a condition affecting the heart
valves following rheumatic fever) is the most important kind of
heart disease and an excessive intake of saturated fat is not a con-
tributory factor. In affluent societies, rheumatic fever has all but
disappeared and CHD is the major problem.
    CHD results from a narrowing of the coronary arteries (these
are the arteries which supply the heart muscle with blood). There
are a number of so-called 'risk factors' that may cause narrowing
(also known as atherosclerosis) and one of them is a high level of
cholesterol in the blood. As a result of arterial narrowing, the
heart receives insufficient amounts of blood.

Angina   At times when the heart beats faster and needs more
blood, for example during physical exercise or in times of stress, a
suffocating pain known as angina may occur. The demand for
blood by the heart exceeds the supply from the coronary arteries.
Such pain is usually experienced over the chest but may sometimes move down the left arm or up into the neck. Angina pain
will usually stop when the person rests.

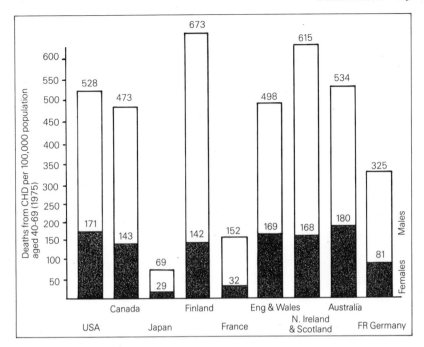

Male and female deaths from CHD in different countries (1975)

Heart attack Angina pain in the chest is usually caused by narrowing of the arteries, which in turn may be the result of cholesterol deposits on the walls of the arteries. If the narrowing is severe or if a blood clot (thrombosis) should form as well as the narrowing, the blood supply to a section of the heart muscle may be completely cut off and this is called a coronary thrombosis or heart attack. Of course, the majority of people who have had a heart attack do recover, but this condition is the single commonest cause of death in middle-aged men in most affluent societies, as well as being a major cause of ill-health and death in both sexes at all ages over 35 years.

Strokes Atherosclerosis can also cause problems to arteries other than those supplying the heart. If the blood supply to the brain is reduced by atherosclerosis, a person is said to have suffered a stroke.

Cramping pain in the calf muscles during exercise (medically known as intermittent claudication) may result when there is an inadequate supply of blood to the affected leg muscles. Both strokes and intermittent claudication appear to be less closely associated with diet, unlike coronary heart disease.

The diagram above gives some idea of the size of the modern epidemic of coronary heart disease which most authorities believe can be substantially controlled by changing the present diet of most affluent countries.

Causes of coronary heart disease

Unfortunately, CHD is not an infection like most other epidemic diseases and does not have a single cause. In several affluent societies, the causes of CHD have been investigated by prospective studies. Such investigations, by definition, involve following a group of many thousands of people over a period of time and taking measurements of various factors thought to be related to CHD, for example, high blood pressure. These studies found that the development of CHD over a period of time (usually five to ten years) can indeed be related to certain measurements. The four most important factors (also called risk factors) are:

- High levels of cholesterol in the blood
- High blood pressure
- Cigarette smoking
- Diabetes.

In addition to these 'major' risk factors, a number of other characteristics have been shown to be associated with CHD. These include obesity, lack of physical exercise and 'stress' (or, more particularly, certain stressful events in a person's life).

Two other blood measurements are thought to be relevant as well: raised levels of blood triglyceride, which may be related to an increase in heart attacks, and reduced levels of high density lipoprotein – you may recall that a high level of HDL helps to prevent cholesterol from being deposited in the walls of arteries.

Does changing the diet really prevent CHD?

Two pieces of evidence so far discussed – first, the link between cholesterol deposition, atherosclerosis and CHD, and second, the effect of polyunsaturated or saturated fat on lowering and raising cholesterol levels respectively – support the belief that changing to a low-fat diet will result in a reduction in CHD.

Further support for this evidence has been obtained by comparing CHD rates in different countries with different eating habits. Differences were found in CHD rates but the only two features which seemed to explain them were the amount of saturated fat eaten and the level of blood cholesterol in the populations of the countries. None of the other risk factors already mentioned (for example smoking, high blood pressure) were found to be important in explaining the differences in CHD rates between populations. It seems that these latter factors only increase the risk of CHD in populations which are already at increased risk because they eat a diet high in saturated fat and have raised blood cholesterol levels. In comparison with earlier epidemic diseases where the infections particularly affected the underprivileged and undernourished, the modern Western epidemic of CHD appears to involve those who are 'overnourished', often overweight and especially those whose diets are high in fat, especially saturated fat, and low in fibre-rich cereals and vegetables. It is chiefly amongst such people that other risk factors seem to be relevant as well.

Direct evidence

All the above facts provide good circumstantial evidence for believing that a dietary change would be beneficial, but the most direct evidence comes from clinical trials which, by definition, involve observing and treating people in controlled conditions.

The most convincing and best-conducted of these trials has been carried out in Oslo, Norway. Middle-aged men in Oslo were offered the opportunity of being tested to see if they were at risk from CHD in the future. Those men found to be at high risk from developing CHD (because they were smokers, had high blood pressure or high blood cholesterol) were divided into two groups. The first group was given intensive dietary education by a special team of researchers; they were recommended to eat the kind of low-fat diet described in this book, and were also told to stop smoking. The second group were given dietary advice, but the advice was not reinforced to the same extent and the participants in this group did not achieve anything like the degree of success attained by those in the first group. As a result, the first group showed a reduction in CHD. These results provide very strong evidence for the benefit of change, at least in people who already have fairly high blood cholesterol levels. Other trials have been carried out on people with lower levels of cholesterol. Unfortunately they were not quite so well conducted as the Oslo study and therefore the results are not so clear cut. Nevertheless, all results suggest a beneficial trend.

What is the ideal level of fat in the diet?

In the typical affluent Western diet, approximately 40 per cent of all daily calories come from fat, 15 per cent from protein and 45 per cent from carbohydrate foods. A diet which will lower blood fats and reduce the risk of CHD is one:

- in which total fat is substantially reduced (to between 30 and 35 per cent of total calories) mainly by reducing saturated fat;
- in which the fat used is polyunsaturated as far as possible;
- in which fibre-rich cereals, vegetables and fruit are increased to 50 per cent of total daily energy to balance the reduction in fat.

Why high-fibre as well?

An increase in fibre-rich foods is recommended for many important reasons and not simply as a substitute for the fatty foods which need to be reduced.

Constipation, a major scourge of people eating a Western diet, is virtually unknown in those people who eat enough dietary fibre. Fibre protects against diverticular disease and irritable bowel syndrome, two very common causes of bowel disturbance in affluent societies. High-fibre diets are used to treat these conditions as well as to help lower blood sugar levels in diabetics. There is also some evidence to suggest that a diet high in cereals, vegetables and fruit may protect against certain cancers and may independently help to lower blood cholesterol. Fifteen years ago, the possible benefits of fibre were first suggested by a very small group of farsighted medical scientists. At the time, most people (including the majority of the medical profession) believed that fibre was merely an obsession of 'health food faddists'. Now there is universal acceptance that it is good for you.

If you make all the dietary changes above, you will also ensure an intake of minerals, vitamins and essential fatty acids without producing a deleterious fall in protein intake, which should remain at about 15 per cent of total energy per day.

These recommendations may be safely followed by the entire population, though they are probably less relevant to those who have already reached a ripe old age and proved their individual resistance to heart disease. Nevertheless, they will still benefit from the fact that such an eating plan is high in fibre. You may already have cut down on fat and increased your fibre intake. But, hopefully, the recipes which follow will help to add variety and interest to your present eating habits.

How can I achieve the ideal diet?
It should be stressed that a balanced low-fat, high-fibre way of eating can be as enjoyable and interesting as any other eating pattern. Indeed the majority of converts believe that it is even more palatable. This book intends to show you how to make the change, if you have not done so already, and to add variety to your cooking if you have already made the basic changes.

The diagram opposite compares an average day's food intake by someone eating a typical British diet to a low-fat alternative. The simplest way of achieving a better balance yourself is to eliminate as many of the 'not advised' foods, in the lists on pages 22–24, as possible and stick to the 'advised' foods. This will help you to achieve a redistribution of calories, so that fewer calories come from fat and more from healthier high-fibre foods. It will also help to reduce body weight in overweight people since many of the 'not advised' foods are also high calorie foods.

Obviously, all dietary estimations have to be calculated to an average of the population and you may well find that you are eating sufficient amounts of fibre already, but it has been worked out that the average person in Britain eats about 20 g of fibre per day. This is low compared to 50–120 g per day estimated for Africans living in rural communities. In Britain during the war, the average fibre intake was 32–40 g fibre and the intake of saturated fats was

	PREVIOUS DIET	LOW-FAT DIET
Breakfast	Cornflakes Whole milk Fried bacon and egg (optional) Toasted white bread or roll Butter Marmalade Coffee or tea with whole milk	Muesli or other wholegrain cereal (see page 110) with blackberries Skimmed milk Grilled lean bacon and tomato (optional) Toasted wholemeal bread, or rolls or oatmeal popovers (see page 98) 1 tsp polyunsaturated margarine Marmalade Coffee or tea with skimmed milk
Mid-morning	Coffee or tea with whole milk Doughnut	Coffee or tea with skimmed milk Nutty oatmeal biscuit (optional) – (see page 99)
Snack lunch	Cheese on toast *or* Meat pie Pickles Ice cream Coffee with whole milk	Beans on wholemeal toast (see pages 107 and 93) *or* Wholemeal spaghetti in meat sauce (see page 107) Fresh fruit Coffee with skimmed milk
Afternoon	Tea or coffee with whole milk Chocolate biscuits	Tea or coffee with skimmed milk Wholesome fingers (optional – see page 98)
Evening	Cream of vegetable soup Beef and kidney casserole with dumplings Sliced carrots tossed in melted butter Creamed potatoes Frozen caramel custards *or* Cheese and biscuits Coffee with cream	Mixed vegetable soup (see page 33) Beef and bean goulash (see page 72) Diced carrots tossed in freshly chopped herbs Jacket potato with yoghurt dressing (see page 100) Blackcurrant cheesecake (see page 89) *or* Fresh fruit Coffee
Bedtime	Whole milk as hot drink Coconut buns	Skimmed milk as a hot drink Slice date and rhubarb cake (optional – see page 99)

COMMENTS:
BREAKFAST Lower overall fat by a) replacing whole milk with skimmed b) limiting amount of polyunsaturated margarine to replace saturated butter fat c) grilling instead of frying. Improve fibre content with wholegrain cereal, bread and fruit.
MID-MORNING Replace high-fat doughnut with satisfying low-fat/high-fibre biscuit. You may not feel hungry enough for mid-morning snack.
LUNCH Replace fatty cheese dish with beans (high-fibre) in tasty sauce *or* replace pie (high-fat) with lean meat in well-flavoured sauce. Spaghetti and fresh vegetables in sauce add fibre.
AFTERNOON Low-fat/high-fibre food (it taken) replaces high-fat snack.
EVENING Replace fatty meal, high in cholesterol, with appetizing meal; high-fibre cereals to replace refined cereals; alternative ways to give food a good flavour.

also low due to restrictions. Vegetarians in the UK at present consume about 42 g of fibre in their daily diet.

It is recommended that adults should gradually increase their fibre intake to at least 30 g per day. It is best to take fibre from a variety of different sources – cereals, fruit and vegetables. Fibre from various types of cooked dried beans (for example, haricot and red kidney) and pectin (from fruit) are particularly useful from the point of view of lowering cholesterol.

The recipes in this book have been specially devised to help you make the change. For many people, the significant change, and perhaps the difficult one, will be a reduction in eating most meats, especially red meat. This is necessary because so many meats are high in fats. Even when the visible fat has been cut off, there is still invisible fat within the flesh. For this reason, you will find that pulses have been used in many of the recipes to compensate for a reduction in meat. Various forms of cooked pulses are particularly useful because they are a good source of protein, high in fibre, and they provide an excellent means of 'extending' the meat. Of course, a vegetarian diet is very easily adapted to the kind of eating pattern we would regard as ideal, but vegetarianism is certainly not essential to achieve the desired food distribution.

For most people wishing to adopt healthier eating habits, with the exception of diabetics and those needing to lose weight, it isn't necessary to calculate your precise calorie intake or to work out the precise quantities of fat, protein and fibre. By following the general principles described here, you will achieve the desired results. Indeed these general principles are sufficient for the great majority of those who have been found to have raised levels of cholesterol and triglyceride, and will help to increase the proportion of high density lipoprotein (see page 13).

If you need to lose weight and cannot achieve the required weight reduction on a low-fat diet alone, the best alternative is actually counting calories using one of the many calorie-counting books presently available; but still continue to concentrate on eating the appropriate types of food.

Alcohol   All forms of alcohol are high in calories and should be restricted if you are overweight. In addition, there is some evidence that alcohol may raise triglyceride levels. Doctors may, therefore, advise the elimination or near elimination of alcohol in those people with established high triglyceride levels. You may also be advised to see a dietitian if a stricter diet plan is necessary.

Other research relevant to the diet and healthy heart story
Perhaps the most interesting recent development in this field is the recognition that certain types of polyunsaturated fats can reduce the tendency of blood to form clots within the arteries, in addition to their well-known property of being able to reduce cholesterol levels. As the formation of clots is a particularly important cause of heart attacks (see page 15), some polyunsaturated fats may indirectly help to reduce the rate of death by coronary thrombosis.

Some recent and fascinating research has shown that Eskimos, who have an especially high intake of a polyunsaturated fat called eicosapentaenoic acid, have a greatly reduced tendency to form clots. Eskimos get their eicosapentaenoic acid from rather unusual sources – seal and whale meat – and unfortunately this fat doesn't appear in many of our ordinary foods. However, it is present in mackerel and other oily fish, so eating a diet high in oily fish may reduce blood clotting in people previously on a more conventional diet.

Further research is looking into the effects of eicosapentaenoic acid and other fats which seem to have exceptional qualities in preventing clots, but at present we are unable to make precise recommendations.

All that can be said is that a moderate intake of the widely available polyunsaturated fats and oils, for example polyunsaturated margarine and sunflower seed oil, is a useful adjunct to a diet low in saturated fat because it helps to lower blood cholesterol levels and may help reduce the tendency to form clots.

Are there any dangers in reducing the fat in the diet?

A low-fat, high-fibre diet is eaten by many populations throughout the world with no ill effects. In theory, reducing the fat in the very young or the very old might reduce calorific and fat-soluble vitamin intake when they are most needed for growth during childhood and in the maintenance of good health in the elderly. There is, however, no evidence that this would be a problem in people following the kind of advice given here, but some authorities have suggested that children under the age of five and the elderly or infirm should have whole milk rather than skimmed milk or skimmed milk products.

The amounts recommended here are well within the safety range eaten by many populations and cannot be anything other than beneficial.

Are there any drugs available if diet alone doesn't reduce blood cholesterol?

There is a whole new range of drugs available that can be used to control blood cholesterol levels if diet alone is unsuccessful. But, once started, they are usually continued for life and most doctors feel very strongly that they should not be started unless people have first tried very hard to achieve the desired result by a change of diet.

For people with an inherited tendency towards raised blood fats, for example familial hypercholesterolaemia (see page 13), drug treatment is usually essential and they should not feel that they have failed if they are unable to achieve a good response on diet alone. There are some drugs in widespread use that have been shown, in a clinical trial, to reduce CHD and prolong life in proportion to the cholesterol-lowering achieved. It is important to continue to eat appropriately even while on drug treatment, since a combination of diet and drugs produces far better results than drug treatment alone.

FOOD TABLES

	ADVISABLE	IN MODERATION	NOT ADVISED
CEREALS	Wholemeal flours Oatmeal Wholegrain rice and pasta Wholemeal breads and crispbreads Porridge Wholegrain breakfast cereals	White flour and white bread Oatcakes White rice and pasta	Fancy breads such as croissants Sugar-coated breakfast cereals
VEGETABLES	All fresh, frozen, canned and dried vegetables – peas, broad beans and sweetcorn Dried beans and lentils are particularly high in fibre Potatoes: baked or boiled in skin; eat with skins whenever possible	Avocado pears Olives	Potato crisps Chips fried in unsuitable oil
FRUIT	Fresh, frozen, dried or canned in natural juice		Fruit canned in heavy syrup
NUTS		English walnuts, hazelnuts Chestnuts, almonds Brazil nuts and peanuts occasionally	Coconut
FISH	All white fish – fresh, frozen, smoked Oily fish such as herring, mackerel, tuna – fresh, frozen canned or smoked	Shellfish occasionally	Fish roe

MEAT	Chicken without skin Turkey without skin Veal Rabbit, game	Ham, beef, pork, lamb Bacon, lean mince Liver and kidney occasionally	Visible fat and skin on meat Sausage, pâté, canned luncheon meat and chopped pork Meat pies Meat paste Duck, goose, streaky bacon Tongue, tripe and other offal meats
EGGS AND DAIRY FOODS	Skimmed milk – fresh or dried Skimmed milk cottage and curd cheese Egg whites Egg yolks: 3 a week only	Fat-reduced cheese Camembert, Brie, Edam-type Small amounts of mature, strong-flavoured cheese such as Parmesan	Whole milk Cream and artificial creams Coffee creamers Stilton and cream cheese
FATS	All fats are strictly limited	Margarine labelled 'high in polyunsaturates' Soya bean oil, safflower oil, sunflower oil, sesame oil, corn oil and olive oil Low-fat margarine spreads	Butter, dripping, suet, lard Margarine not 'high in poly-unsaturates' Peanut oil, groundnut oil, palm oil Vegetable oils of unknown origin Peanut butter
MADE-UP DISHES	Fruity and other low-fat puddings such as sorbet, jelly Skimmed milk puddings and sauces Cakes, biscuits and pastry made with wholemeal flour and suitable fat	Puddings, cakes, biscuits and pastry made with white flour but with suitable fat Home-made ice cream Water biscuits, matzos Proprietary low-fat/low-calorie salad dressings	Wholemilk, canned and proprietary puddings Cakes, biscuits, and sauces made with wholemilk, excess egg yolks and unsuitable fats Rich, high-fat ice cream Savoury cheese biscuits Mayonnaise

(continued)

	ADVISABLE	IN MODERATION	NOT ADVISED
SOUPS	Beans, lentils and peas with other vegetables and wholegrain cereals Fat-free stocks and consommés	Packet and canned clear soups	Cream soups
SUGAR, CONFECTIONARY AND PRESERVES		Sugar, syrup, honey Boiled sweets, fruit pastilles, marshmallows, Turkish delight Jam, marmalade	Chocolate, toffees, fudge, butterscotch Lemon curd, mincemeat
FLAVOURING SEASONING	Herbs and spices and most condiments	Salt, salted vegetable and meat extracts, salted stock cubes	
DRINKS	Tea, coffee, fruit juice Mineral water, other soft drinks	Wines, spirits, beer, cider	

COOKING FOR A HEALTHY HEART

Weights and measures

In all the recipes, calculations are based on metric weights and measures, but wherever practical these have been expressed in household measures or descriptions. Where this is not possible, the nearest equivalent in Imperial weights (pounds and ounces) has been given.

The tablespoon measurement used throughout the book equals 15 ml and the teaspoon 5 ml; both are level unless otherwise stated. Check the size of your spoons to ensure success.

Australian users should remember that as their tablespoon has been converted to 20 ml, and is therefore larger than the tablespoon measurement used in the recipes in this book, they should use 3 5ml tsp where instructed to use 1 15 ml tbsp.

Changing the quantities
The quantities used in most of the recipes can be halved to accommodate the smaller family. Where only a single serving is required, the remainder can usually be reheated a day or two later or deep-frozen. Casserole-type recipes are particularly good for reheating.

Calories and joules
The kilocalorie (kcal) is used to express the energy content of food. The metric equivalent – kilojoule (kJ) – is also given. Fibre and fat values have been rounded to the nearest gram.

Ingredients

We recommend that you use the following ingredients in your cooking:
- Skimmed milk or reconstituted dried skimmed milk to replace whole milk in cooking.
- Cheeses made from skimmed milk, such as cottage cheese and quark (quarg), and curd cheeses (provided they are labelled as low-fat).
- Curd cheese sweetened and used in place of whipped cream in fruit flans, tartlets and so on (see page 92).
- Fromage blanc, instead of pouring custard or pouring cream when serving cooked or canned fruit.
- Other permitted cheese in cooking (see chart on page 23);

choose mature cheese with a strong flavour – for example Parmesan – so that much smaller quantities can be used to give flavour.

- Low-fat plain yoghurt to replace sour cream in recipes such as goulash, to make simple low-fat salad dressings (see page 100) and for giving body to sauces.
- Fruit yoghurt: shop around for yoghurts which are very low in fat, have no added sugar and have added vitamins.
- Polyunsaturated margarines and low-fat spreads, and polyunsaturated oils, such as soya bean oil, safflower oil, sunflower oil, sesame oil, corn oil and monounsaturated olive oil; use polyunsaturated margarine or low-fat margarine spread with wholemeal flour for making cakes, biscuits and pastry; use the permitted oils for making French dressing (recipes, see page 101) and marinades.
- Low-calorie salad cream for slimmers to spread on sandwiches, filled rolls etc. Some proprietary salad creams have less than ¼ the number of calories in the same weight of butter or polyunsaturated margarine.
- Lean meat and trim off all visible fat and skin before cooking; it is better to choose fish and poultry more often than red meat.
- Combine meat with pulses, other vegetables and cereals so that less meat is used.
- Chicken can always be substituted for turkey if it is easier or more economical, and vice-versa.
- Suitable textured vegetable proteins (TVP), which are very low in fat, to replace meat in some recipes.
- Wholemeal flour, but make sure it is 100 per cent – that is, unrefined.
- Fresh fruit and vegetables with the skins left on, if possible. Frozen and canned may be substituted but check that sugar has not been added.
- Herbs and spices: vary the amounts to suit individual tastes. The quantities given are usually for fresh herbs; if using dried herbs, use about ⅓ of the quantity stated.
- Sugar-free sweeteners: for those who need to lose weight or are specifically ordered to cut out sugar, artificial sweeteners may be used. The recipes have therefore been calculated using them, giving sugar equivalents where necessary.

Cooking and preparation

- Read the labels carefully on packet and canned foods to make sure the ingredients are suitable to include in the recipe.
- Grill, bake, steam, poach or boil in place of frying.
- When mince is required in a recipe, buy lean meat in one piece and mince it at home.
- Skim off any visible fat from stocks, soups and stews. If food is

cooked the day before it is to be eaten, any hard fat which has collected on the surface should be removed.

- Drain oil from canned fish or look for varieties canned in brine.
- To make sauces, blend the thickening agent with the liquid and bring to the boil stirring, rather than melting the fat, adding the thickener and making a roux.
- Glaze pies and pastry with skimmed milk rather than egg and milk.
- Wholemeal flours vary in the amount of liquid they will absorb, so in baking, add 1–2 tbsp extra water if the consistency is too stiff.
- Where self-raising flour is stated in a plain cake mixture, baking powder may be added to unrefined wholemeal flour instead: use 30 g/1 oz baking powder to 450 g /1 lb flour.
- When rolling out wholemeal pastry, roll between polythene or grease-proof paper to overcome the problem of making holes in the dough.
- The amount of vegetables in recipes may be increased to extend the recipes – remember that beans and lentils are particularly good sources of fibre for people with raised levels of blood cholesterol.
- In recipes which feature stock, stock cubes can be used instead. As these are fairly salty, the amount of salt in the recipe should be reduced. Where stock flavour is not specified, use whichever you like, for example, a vegetarian stock cube could be used.
- All soups will keep for two days in the refrigerator.
- Seasoning with salt should always be light.

Cooking equipment
- Use good quality non-stick pans, casseroles and baking dishes to reduce use of cooking oil and fat to a minimum. Other baking dishes can be lined with non-stick paper.
- When baking larger pieces of meat and some vegetables, use roasting bags or foil covering to retain the juices and keep the food tender. The meat may be placed on a rack before covering with foil.
- Using an electric blender for processing food is better than sieving, because it ensures that valuable fibre remains in the food. Do not blend food to too fine a purée. If you use a Moulimill or other type of sieve instead of a blender, make sure no fibre-rich residue remains in the utensil.
- Shop around for a clay pot suitable for cooking jacket potatoes on a gas ring.
- Use a Continental cheese slicer to make wafer-thin slices of hard cheese.
- Perforated cooking spoons are recommended, as they help to drain off the fat used in cooking.

Pulses

Many supermarkets now stock a wide variety of dried, frozen and canned pulses. Unusual types can be found in Oriental food shops, delicatessens and healthfood stores.

Canned beans may replace cooked beans in recipes, providing no sugar has been used in canning.

You can vary the type of beans specified in the recipes without significantly affecting the analyses – except soya beans which have different dietary constituents.

Soaking   Wash thoroughly and soak in cold water overnight. Alternatively, place in a pan of cold water, bring to the boil and cook for 2–3 minutes. Remove from the heat, cover and leave to soak for 1 hour. The weight of the soaked beans is about double their dry weight. In the recipes, where the bean weights are expressed as a certain amount, soaked, this is the weight before soaking – in other words, the dry weight. Cooked beans weigh approximately double their dry weight.

Cooking   Put the beans in a large pan with plenty of water. Boil rapidly for 10 minutes. Cover and simmer gently until soft, stirring occasionally to ensure even cooking. The cooking time varies according to the type and even those of the same type can take different times, depending on their age and the amount being cooked. If you cook pulses frequently, you may consider it worth while buying a pressure-cooker as this reduces the cooking times.

Many of the smaller varieties, lentils and aduki beans, for example, can be cooked without soaking, but allow a little longer for cooking.

up to 30 minutes
(10 minutes in pressure-cooker):

aduki beans
British field beans
mung beans
peas
split peas
split red lentils

30 minutes to 1 hour
(15–20 minutes in pressure-cooker):

black-eyed beans
black beans
barlotti beans
cannellini beans
flageolot beans
Continental lentils
ful madames
lima beans

1 to 2 hours *(½–1 hour in pressure cooker)*:	broad beans butter beans chick peas haricot beans speckled Mexican beans red kidney beans
3 to 4 hours *(1–1½ hours in pressure-cooker)*:	soya beans

Leave the seasoning until cooking is almost complete, as the addition of salt, vinegar, lemon juice or tomatoes tends to toughen the skin and prevent cooking.

Cooked beans are versatile: they will keep in the refrigerator for 3–4 days, or for a month or more in the deep-freezer if mixed with onions, etc (or a year if cooked alone). Many bean dishes can be reheated and served again.

To save time and energy, cook larger quantities than stated in the recipes and use leftovers later for quick snacks, soups, salads and so on. Herbs and spices can be varied and different sauces added, such as Worcester, soy, low-calorie ketchup and salad dressings. Beans can also be heated through in home-made sauces (see pages 101–2) and served with brown rice, wholemeal pasta or on wholemeal toast, with added fresh vegetables or accompanied by other vegetable dishes.

Brown rice
There are three principal varieties of brown rice. Long-grain e.g. Patna – the grains remain separate and fluff up when cooked. It is used to accompany savoury dishes or it may form part of the dish. Round or short-grain – is used for making rice puddings as the grains are inclined to become sticky and clump together when cooked. Medium-grain rice with rounded ends – varieties grown in Italy and Spain are used for making risotto and paella, but are difficult to find elsewhere. Substitute with long-grain brown rice, if necessary. Shop around for quick-cooking brown rice.

Brown rice has more flavour than white rice, and has a higher vitamin and mineral content, although the B vitamin, Thiamin, needed by the body to utilize carbohydrate will be lost in the cooking water unless the correct proportions of rice to liquid are used. These are – 1 measure of rice to 2 measures of boiling water and 1 tsp of salt per 600 ml/1 pt water or stock.

Cooking   If there are cooking instructions on the packet, follow them: some varieties of brown rice require more than twice the quantity of water to rice.

Bring the measured amount of water to the boil, add the rice (washed, if necessary) and salt, return to simmering point. Stir once, cover tightly and simmer steadily for about 40 minutes or until the grains are just tender.

Leave alone when cooking – if the lid is lifted, steam will escape and slow down the cooking time and, if stirred, the grains will break releasing the starch inside, making the rice sticky and lumpy.

If the water has not been completely absorbed, leave uncovered over the heat for a few minutes.

Cooked rice can then be gently fluffed up with a fork, or copy the Chinese and leave the rice tightly covered on the lowest possible heat for 10 minutes. It is a great advantage to have a heavy pan for this.

Cooking in the oven   Use the same proportions of rice to water. Put the rice and salt in a casserole, stir in the boiling water and cook in the oven for approximately 1–1¼ hours at 180°C/350°F/ gas 4.

Reheating   It is often convenient to cook a larger quantity than required – covered, it will keep in the refrigerator for a week. To reheat, place in a pan with a little water and put over a gentle heat, giving an occasional stir; or place in an ovenproof dish with a little water, cover tightly and heat in the oven for about 20 minutes.

Wholemeal pasta
There are about a dozen varieties of plain wholemeal pasta shapes. They can be bought in supermarkets and healthfood stores.

Wholemeal pasta is suitable to include in your diet as it is high in carbohydrate, low in fat and has a good fibre content. It has more flavour and a firmer texture than ordinary pasta.

Pasta can be treated as a main course or snack meal, or used in place of potatoes to accompany meat and fish dishes. It is also delicious in soups or cooked and added to salads. Try serving pasta with some of the sauces on pages 00–000.

Cooking   If there are cooking instructions on the packet, it is wise to follow them. Allow plenty of boiling water to prevent the pasta sticking together: approximately 4 litres (6–8 pints) water for each 450 g/1 lb pasta. Slowly add the pasta to the boiling water so that the water does not go off the boil. Stir with a fork to ensure it does not stick together or to the pan, and cook steadily, uncovered, until just tender, but still firm. The cooking time will vary from approximately 8–18 minutes depending on the size and freshness of the pasta. Drain well.

SOUPS AND STARTERS

LIGHT SOUPS

Onion soup

Serves 4
Each serving: 70 kcal/290 kJ, 5 g fibre, 1 g fat

2 large onions, roughly chopped
celery salt
pepper
850 ml/1½ pints beef stock

75 ml/5 tbsp dried skimmed milk
4 tbsp natural bran flakes
2 tbsp dried mixed peppers
½ tbsp chopped basil

Put the onions, seasoning and stock in a saucepan and simmer for 10–15 minutes, or until tender. Remove from the heat and stir in the milk, blended with a little water. Purée the soup in a blender, leaving a few small pieces of onion visible. Stir in the bran and mixed peppers. Return to the rinsed saucepan and bring to the boil. Adjust the seasoning, add the basil and serve.

Mixed vegetable soup

Serves 4
Each serving: 60 kcal/250 kJ, 3 g fibre, 0 g fat

1 medium-sized carrot, diced
1 medium-sized onion, diced
125 g/4½ oz potato, diced
100 g/3½ oz swede, diced
garlic salt

pepper
850 ml/1½ pints stock
¼ small cabbage, finely shredded
150 ml/¼ pint skimmed milk
1 tbsp chopped parsley

Put all the vegetables, except the cabbage, in a saucepan with the seasoned stock and simmer for 30 minutes, or until the vegetables are tender. Add the cabbage and continue cooking for 10 minutes. Add the milk, bring back to the simmer and add the parsley. Adjust seasoning if necessary and serve.

Variations
Use other vegetables in season allowing approximately 500 g/ 18 oz vegetables to 850 ml/1½ pints stock.

Wholemeal pasta soup

Serves 4
Each serving: 30 kcal/130 kJ, 2 g fibre, negligible fat

850 ml/1½ pints stock
1 medium-sized carrot, diced
30 g/1 oz wholemeal pasta

½ tsp garlic salt
seasoning
1 tbsp chopped parsley

Put the stock in a saucepan and bring to the boil. Add the carrot, pasta and salt and simmer, covered, for 10–20 minutes (depending on type of pasta) or until the pasta is cooked. Add the parsley, adjust the seasoning if necessary and serve.

MAIN COURSE SOUPS

Italian vegetable soup

Serves 4, twice
Each serving: 240 kcal/1010 kJ, 14 g fibre, 2 g fat

225 g/8 oz haricot beans, soaked (see page 28)
2 litres/3½ pints water
1 medium-sized onion, chopped
2 cloves garlic, crushed
2 young leeks, chopped
2 stalks celery, sliced
2 medium-sized carrots, sliced
3 courgettes, sliced
400 g/14 oz canned tomatoes, chopped with juice
375 g/13 oz potatoes, chopped un-peeled

¼ small cabbage, finely shredded
100 g/3½ oz frozen or fresh peas
170 g/6 oz wholemeal pasta, e.g. spaghetti broken into short lengths
4 tsp fresh basil, marjoram and thyme, chopped (or 1–2 tsp dried mixed herbs)
seasoning
6 tbsp chopped parsley
30 g/1 oz Parmesan cheese, grated

Put the beans and water in a saucepan and simmer for 20–30 minutes. Add the onion, garlic, leeks, celery and carrots and simmer for a further 30 minutes. Add the courgettes, tomatoes and potatoes and continue simmering for 30 minutes. Add the cabbage, peas, pasta, mixed herbs and seasoning and continue simmering for 20 minutes or until the pasta is tender.

Just before serving, stir in the parsley. Spoon into bowls and sprinkle the cheese over the top.

Italian vegetable soup (*top*); Scottish lentil broth (*centre*, see page 35); Scandinavian pea soup (*bottom*, see page 35)
Overleaf: Chicken or turkey and rice salad with grapes (*top*, see page 36); Salad Niçoise (*centre*, see page 37); Red cabbage and chestnut salad (*bottom*, see page 39)

Scottish lentil broth   See photograph, page 33

Serves 4, twice
Each serving: 190 kcal/800 kJ, 9 g fibre, negligible fat

400 g/14 oz red lentils
2 litres/3½ pints water
1 ham bone, cracked or about 8 bacon
*   rinds*
2 medium-sized carrots, diced
1 medium-sized onion, chopped
1 medium-sized leek, chopped

200 g/7 oz cabbage, finely shredded
1 medium–large potato, diced
1 bouquet garni (parsley, bay leaf
*   and thyme)*
seasoning
4 tbsp chopped parsley

Put the lentils, water and ham bone or bacon rinds into a large saucepan. Bring to the boil and boil for 10 minutes removing any scum as it rises. Reduce the heat to low, cover the pan and simmer for 20 minutes.

Stir in the vegetables, bouquet garni and seasoning, and simmer, covered, for about 30 minutes or until the vegetables are cooked. Remove the ham bone and bouquet garni. Stir in the parsley, adjust the seasoning if necessary and serve.

Alternatively, this soup may be put through a blender, but do not blend too finely.

Note: Soaked brown lentils, dried beans or peas may be substituted for red lentils. Adjust cooking times from information on page 28.

Scandinavian pea soup   See photograph, page 33

Serves 4, twice
Each serving: 200 kcal/840 kJ, 13 g fibre, 1 g fat

500 g/18 oz dried peas, soaked (see
*   page 28)*
2 litres/3½ pints water
pork bones or a cracked ham bone
4 small onions, chopped
4 medium-sized carrots, sliced

4 stalks celery, sliced
sprig thyme (or 2 tsp dried thyme)
1 tsp dried marjoram (optional)
seasoning
4 tbsp chopped parsley

Put the peas, water and bones into a large saucepan. Bring to the boil and boil for 10 minutes. Reduce the heat, cover the pan and simmer for 30 minutes. Add the vegetables, the thyme and marjoram, if used, and return to the boil. Simmer for about 30 minutes or until all the vegetables are cooked.

Remove the bones and vegetables. Mash the peas with a spoon or process to a coarse purée in a blender and return to the rinsed saucepan. Dice the vegetables and add with the seasoning to the puréed peas. The soup should be very thick.

Reheat, stir in the parsley and serve, accompanied by rye bread or rye crispbread.

SALADS

MAIN COURSE SALADS

Chicken, ham and apple salad

Serves 4
Each serving: 210 kcal/880 kJ, 10 g fibre, 4 g fat

1 medium-sized red apple, cored and diced
1 medium-sized green apple, cored and diced
15 ml/1 tbsp lemon juice
100 g/3½ oz cooked chicken † meat, diced
100 g/3½ oz cooked lean ham, diced
200 g/7 oz frozen peas, cooked
100 g/3½ oz chestnuts, cooked, skinned and finely chopped*

3 large stalks celery, chopped
30 g/1 oz sultanas, chopped
1 fairly large head of chicory

Dressing
60 ml/4 tbsp orange juice
150 ml/¼ pint low-fat plain yoghurt
finely grated rind of 1 orange
seasoning

Place the diced apples in a large bowl, add the lemon juice and stir until evenly coated. Mix in the remaining salad ingredients, except the chicory.

Combine the dressing ingredients together and stir into the salad. Arrange the chicory blades like a sunflower on a serving dish and pile the salad mixture in the centre.

†Turkey may be substituted for chicken.
*Canned sugar-free or reconstituted dried chestnuts may be used.

Chicken or turkey and rice salad with grapes
See photograph, page 34

Serves 4
Each serving: 210 kcal/880 kJ, 4 g fibre, 6 g fat

200 g/7 oz cooked chicken or turkey pieces, diced
200 g/7 oz cooked brown rice (see page 29)
4 tbsp natural bran flakes
60 g/2 oz mixed green and black grapes, halved and seeded

150 ml/¼ pint Basic yoghurt dressing (see page 100)
lettuce leaves, shredded
15 g/½ oz flaked almonds, lightly toasted

Combine the chicken, rice, bran and grapes with the salad dressing. Place the lettuce in a salad bowl and pile the chicken and rice mixture on top. Scatter toasted almonds over the salad before serving.

Sweet and sour pork salad

Serves 4
Each serving: 200 kcal/840 kJ, 9 g fibre, 4 g fat

225 g/8 oz lean cooked pork, cubed
300 g/10½ oz canned red kidney beans or cooked beans (see page 28)
6 stalks celery, chopped
2 spring onions, chopped
lettuce leaves
1 medium-sized green pepper, cut into rings

Sweet and sour dressing
60 ml/4 tbsp low-calorie tomato ketchup
15 ml/1 tbsp wine vinegar
5 ml/1 tsp lemon juice
5 ml/1 tsp soy sauce

Combine the pork, beans, celery and spring onions. Combine the dressing ingredients together, then stir into the salad ingredients. Line a dish with lettuce leaves, pile the salad on top and decorate with pepper rings.

Salade Niçoise   See photograph, page 34

Serves 4
Each serving: 180 kcal/760 kJ, 5 g fibre, 11 g fat

1 large crisp lettuce
100 g/3½ oz canned tuna fish in brine, drained and flaked
1 tbsp drained capers
60 g/2 oz black olives, stoned and halved
1 large green pepper, sliced

½ large cucumber, sliced
4 large firm tomatoes, sliced
2 hard-boiled eggs, sliced
30 ml/2 tbsp French dressing (see page 101)
60 g/1 small can anchovy fillets

Tear the lettuce leaves in half and place in the bottom of a large salad bowl. Arrange the tuna fish over the lettuce with the capers and half the olives. Add the pepper, cucumber, tomatoes and eggs. Lightly toss with the French dressing. Garnish with anchovy fillets and remaining olives.

Lentil and garlic salad

Serves 4
Each serving: 220 kcal/920 kJ, 9 g fibre, 4 g fat

200 g/7 oz whole lentils
90 ml/6 tbsp bottled low-calorie

vinaigrette dressing
1 clove garlic, crushed

4 spring onions, chopped
4 medium-sized tomatoes, chopped
2 stalks celery, chopped
2 tbsp chopped parsley
seasoning

crisp lettuce leaves
30 g/1 oz black olives, stoned and
* quartered*
1 hard-boiled egg, chopped

Cook the lentils (see page 28). Mix the lentils with the dressing and garlic while still hot and leave to cool. Add the remaining ingredients and mix well. Arrange the lettuce leaves in a bowl. Spoon the salad on top and garnish with the olives and egg.

Haricot beans in green dressing

Serves 4
Each serving: 300 kcal/1260 kJ, 22 g fibre, 6 g fat

300 g/10½ oz haricot beans, soaked
* (see page 28)*
1 large Spanish onion, chopped
1 clove garlic, crushed
1 bay leaf
1 litre/1¾ pints water
1 medium-sized green pepper, chopped
1 large bunch spring onions, green and
* white parts, chopped*

150 ml/¼ pint Green dressing (see
* page 101)*
crisp lettuce leaves
60 g/2 oz canned anchovy fillets,
* drained and chopped*
60 g/2 oz black olives, halved and
* stoned*
1 hard-boiled egg, chopped

Drain the beans and put them in a saucepan with the onion, garlic, bay leaf and water and bring to the boil. Lower the heat, cover the pan and simmer until the beans are tender (see page 28). Drain and return to the pan. Stir in the pepper and spring onions and set aside to cool.

Stir in the dressing and mix well. Line a serving dish with crisp lettuce leaves, spoon the haricot beans on top and garnish with anchovies, olives and egg.

ACCOMPANIMENT SALADS

Cabbage and raisin salad

Serves 4
Each serving: 110 kcal/460 kJ, 4 g fibre, 4 g fat

250 g/9 oz white cabbage, shredded
100 g/3½ oz fennel or celery, thinly
* sliced*
1 medium-sized green pepper, sliced

60 g/2 oz green grapes, halved and
* seeded*
60 g/2 oz raisins, chopped

Dressing
15 ml/1 tbsp polyunsaturated oil
30 ml/2 tbsp dry white wine
30 ml/2 tbsp white wine vinegar

garlic salt
pepper
1 tsp prepared mustard

Mix all the salad ingredients together in a bowl. Combine the dressing ingredients together and add to the salad, tossing well. Leave for 15–20 minutes before serving.

Sweetcorn, rice and pepper salad

Serves 4   See photograph, page 64
Each serving: 190 kcal/800 kJ, 6 g fibre, 5 g fat

100 g/3½ oz long-grain brown rice
150 g/5 oz sweetcorn kernels, cooked
100 g/3½ oz frozen peas, cooked
1 medium-sized red pepper, chopped
1 bunch watercress or lettuce leaves

Dressing
15 ml/1 tbsp polyunsaturated oil
60 ml/4 tbsp wine vinegar
½ tsp prepared mustard
onion salt
pepper

Cook the rice (see page 29). First make the dressing. Combine all the ingredients together and stir into the rice while still warm. Leave to cool. Stir in the corn, peas and red pepper. Line the salad bowl with watercress or lettuce leaves and pile in the rice mixture. Chill before serving.

Red cabbage and chestnut salad

Serves 4   See photograph, page 34
Each serving: 140 kcal/590 kJ, 7 g fibre, 1 g fat

200 g/7 oz red cabbage, finely shredded
200 g/7 oz chestnuts, skinned, cooked and finely chopped*
1 medium-sized eating apple, grated unpeeled

1 medium-sized onion, finely grated
30 g/1 oz raisins, chopped
60 ml/4 tbsp Basic yoghurt dressing (see page 100)
3 tbsp chopped chives

Blanch the cabbage in boiling water for 2 minutes, place in a colander and thoroughly rinse in cold water. Transfer to a salad bowl, add the chestnuts, grated apple, onion and raisins and mix well. Spoon the dressing over the salad and toss. Garnish with the chopped chives, set aside for 30–60 minutes in the refrigerator and serve.

This salad, stored in a covered container, keeps well in the refrigerator for a few days.

*Canned sugar-free or reconstituted dried chestnuts can be used.

Russian salad

Serves 4
Each serving: 100 kcal/420 kJ, 6 g fibre, negligible fat

150 g/5 oz cooked potatoes, diced
150 g/5 oz cooked beetroot, diced
150 g/5 oz cooked haricot beans
  (see page 28)

150 g/5 oz cooked carrots, diced
60 ml/4 tbsp Basic yoghurt dressing
  (see page 100)
3 tbsp chopped parsley, or other
  mixed fresh herbs

Mix all the ingredients together, reserving 1 tbsp of parsley or herbs to sprinkle over the top.

Cracked wheat salad

Serves 4
Each serving: 140 kcal/590 kJ, 5 g fibre, 5 g fat

100 g/3½ oz burgul (cracked wheat)
4 spring onions, chopped
4 tbsp chopped parsley
3 tbsp chopped mint
3 medium-sized tomatoes, chopped

Dressing:
15 ml/1 tbsp sunflower or other
  polyunsaturated oil

15 ml/1 tbsp lemon juice
seasoning

Garnish:
crisp lettuce leaves
¼ medium cucumber, sliced
10 black olives, stoned

Soak the burgul (cracked wheat) in water for 15 minutes. Drain and squeeze dry. Add the remaining ingredients and mix well. Line a serving plate with lettuce. Pile the salad in the centre and garnish with the cucumber and olives.

Potato salad

Serves 4
Each serving: 100 kcal/420 kJ, 1 g fibre, negligible fat

450 g/1 lb cooked potatoes, diced
60 ml/4 tbsp Basic yoghurt dressing
  (see page 100)

1 tbsp finely chopped onion
1 tbsp chopped parsley

Use waxy potatoes if possible. Mix the cold potatoes with the dressing, onion and chopped parsley. Serve.

VEGETABLE DISHES

ACCOMPANIMENT DISHES

Summer vegetable casserole

Serves 4
Each serving: 100 kcal/420 kJ, 8 g fibre, 3 g fat

15 ml/1 tbsp polyunsaturated oil
1 small onion, coarsely chopped
1 small courgette, diced
1 small green chilli, seeded and finely chopped or a good pinch powdered chilli or cayenne pepper
1 clove garlic, crushed
2 medium-sized tomatoes, coarsely chopped

200 g/7 oz young fresh or frozen broad beans
200 g/7 oz fresh or frozen runner beans, sliced
100 ml/3½ fl oz water
seasoning
200 g/7 oz fresh or canned sweetcorn kernels

Heat the oil in a saucepan. Add the onion, courgette, chilli, garlic, tomatoes and beans and fry gently, stirring occasionally, until the onion is soft. Add the water and seasoning and simmer for 10–15 minutes or until the beans are almost cooked. Stir in the corn and continue to cook for a further 5 minutes, or until the vegetables are tender. Serve hot.

Spinach with paprika and croutons

Serves 4
Each serving: 110 kcal/450 kJ, 15 g fibre, 2 g fat

450 g/1 lb* frozen spinach, thawed
seasoning (garlic salt may be used)
pinch grated nutmeg
90 ml/6 tbsp low-fat plain yoghurt

60 g/2 oz sliced wholemeal bread, toasted
paprika

Place the spinach in a saucepan with 1–2 spoonfuls of water, salt and pepper and cook slowly, stirring occasionally, for 10–15 minutes. Drain thoroughly to remove any moisture, then stir in the nutmeg and yoghurt. Cut the toast into diamond shapes, dip into the paprika and use to decorate the spinach.

*If using fresh spinach allow 900 g/2 lb for 4 people.

Tomatoes Provençal

See photograph, page 51

Serves 4
Each serving: 100 kcal/420 kJ, 5 g fibre, 4 g fat

4 large firm Spanish-type tomatoes
2 tbsp chopped parsley
¼ tsp dried thyme (optional)
¼ tsp dried basil (optional)
1 clove garlic, crushed

seasoning
2 tbsp finely-chopped spring onions
85 g/3 oz wholemeal bread, crumbed
15 ml/1 tbsp polyunsaturated oil

Heat the oven to 200°C/400°F/gas 6.

Cut the tomatoes in half and scoop out the pulp. Mix the chopped tomato pulp with the herbs, garlic, seasoning, spring onions and half of the breadcrumbs. Pile into the tomato shells. Sprinkle the remaining breadcrumbs and then the oil, on top. Place in an ovenproof dish and bake for 15–20 minutes. Alternatively, cook slowly under a low grill. Just before serving, turn up the grill and brown the top.

Dieters' ratatouille

Serves 4
Each serving: 40 kcal/170 kJ, 4 g fibre, negligible fat

1 medium-sized onion, sliced
1 aubergine, sliced
1 medium-sized green pepper, sliced into rings
1 medium-sized red pepper, sliced into rings

2 courgettes or small marrows, sliced
1 tsp garlic salt
pepper
pinch dried thyme
300 g/10½ oz canned tomatoes, chopped with juice

Heat the oven to 190°C/375°F/gas 5.

Place the onion, aubergine, peppers and courgettes, or marrows in a non-stick ovenproof casserole. Add the garlic salt, pepper and thyme to the tomato liquid and mix well. Pour the tomatoes and liquid over the vegetables in the casserole and cook in the oven for 30–45 minutes or until the vegetables are tender but not disintegrating.

Try making this ratatouille with other vegetables. Serve hot or cold.

Rotkohl (spiced red cabbage)

Serves 4
Each serving: 70 kcal/290 kJ, 5 g fibre, 1 g fat

300 g/10½ oz red cabbage, finely sliced

5 ml/1 tsp polyunsaturated margarine
250 ml/9 fl oz cold water

2 small onions, chopped
4 cloves
1 bay leaf
30 ml/2 tbsp red wine

seasoning
300 g/10½ oz cooking apples, cored
* and sliced*

Blanch the cabbage in boiling water for 2 minutes and drain. Melt the margarine in a saucepan. Toss the cabbage in the margarine for about 5 minutes. Add the water, onions, cloves, bay leaf, wine and seasoning and simmer for 20 minutes. Add the apple and simmer for 10 minutes. Remove the cloves and bay leaf and serve.

Okra Olympia

Serves 4
Each serving: 130 kcal/550 kJ, 10 g fibre, 7 g fat

680 g/1½ lb fresh, frozen or canned
* okra, trimmed and sliced*
30 ml/2 tbsp polyunsaturated oil
3 medium-sized onions, finely chopped
5 medium-sized tomatoes, chopped

½ lemon, sliced
seasoning
1 tbsp oregano
¼ tsp dark brown sugar
90 ml/6 tbsp water

If the okra is fresh, blanch it briefly in a pan of boiling salted water and drain. Heat the oil in a saucepan and cook the onions gently for about 10 minutes. Add the okra, if fresh, and cook for 5 minutes (omit this stage if using frozen or canned okra). Add the remaining ingredients, cover and simmer for 20 minutes. Season and serve accompanied by hot wholemeal toast.

Potatoes with onions

Serves 4
Each serving: 250 kcal/1050 kJ, 7 g fibre, negligible fat

4 medium-sized onions, thinly sliced
1 kg/2¼ lb potatoes, cut in 5 mm
* (¼ in) slices*

pepper
½ tsp dried mixed herbs
1 beef stock cube

Arrange the onion rings and potato slices in layers in a fireproof casserole and sprinkle with a little pepper and the herbs. Dissolve the stock cube in water and add to the casserole to a depth of 2½ cm/1 inch. Cover and simmer for 30–35 minutes until the potatoes are tender.

For variety, 1–2 tbsp of powdered soup blended in water may be substituted for the beef cube.

RICE AND PASTA

RICE DISHES

Spicy pilau

Serves 4
Each serving: 340 kcal/1430 kJ, 8 g fibre, 5 g fat

225 g/8 oz long-grain brown rice
600 ml/1 pint good meat stock, boiling
15 ml/1 tbsp tomato purée
1 medium-sized onion, chopped
¼ tsp each ground ginger, cloves, cinnamon and cumin
1 tsp salt (omit if stock cube is used)
pepper
1 medium-sized red pepper, diced
1 medium-sized carrot, diced and cooked
150 g/5 oz fresh or frozen peas
200 g/7 oz lean cooked lamb, chopped

Heat the oven to 180°C/350°F/gas 4.

Put the rice, stock, tomato purée, onion, spices and seasoning into a deep ovenproof dish and mix well. Cover with a tight-fitting lid and cook in the oven for 1 hour. Stir in the red pepper, carrot, peas and lamb, cover and heat for a further 15 minutes. The rice should be dry and flaky – fluff up with a fork before serving.

Brown rice with orange

Serves 2
Each serving: 130 kcal/550 kJ, 3 g fibre, negligible fat

500 g/18 oz cooked long-grain brown rice (see page 29)
1 large orange, sectioned and chopped
rind of 1 orange, cut into matchsticks
1 tbsp chopped tarragon
1 tbsp chopped chervil (optional)*
2 tbsp bottled oil-free French dressing

While the rice is cooking, scrub the orange, remove the orange part of the rind and cut into fine strips. Soak in boiling water for 10 minutes. (Alternatively, grate the rind).

Mix all the ingredients together and serve hot or cold as an accompaniment to a main dish.

*Other seasonings may be substituted, depending on the dish it is to accompany – for example, soy sauce, coriander or lemon juice if the rice is to accompany a Chinese or Indian dish.

Indonesian rice

Serves 4
Each serving: 280 kcal/1180 kJ, 4 g fibre, 5 g fat

200 g/7 oz long-grain brown rice
2 shallots or small onions, finely chopped
1 clove garlic, crushed
1 tsp ground coriander
½ tsp ground cumin
¼ tsp chilli powder

1 tsp salt (omit if stock cube is used)
pepper
500 ml/18 fl oz chicken stock
100 g/3½ oz canned shrimps, drained
100 g/3½ oz cooked chicken, diced
1 egg, beaten

Heat oven to 180°C/350°F/gas 4.

Place the rice, shallots, garlic, spices and seasoning in an oven-proof dish and add the stock. Cover and cook in the oven for 1 hour. Stir in the shrimps and chicken and return to the oven for 15 minutes.

Meanwhile, make a flat omelette with the beaten egg in a small non-stick frying pan. Allow to cook, then shred into noodle-like strips.

Remove the rice from the oven, fluff up with a fork (it should be dry and flaky), garnish with strips of omelette and serve.

Turkish pilaff

Serves 4
Each serving: 410 kcal/1720 kJ, 15 g fibre, 4 g fat

200 g/7 oz long-grain brown rice
500 ml/18 fl oz chicken stock, boiling
bouquet garni (bay leaf, parsley and a sprig of thyme)
seasoning
100 g/3½ oz seedless raisins, roughly chopped

300 g/10½ oz cooked or canned chick peas
1 medium-sized green pepper, chopped
3 medium-sized tomatoes, chopped
chopped mixed fresh herbs
300 ml/½ pint low-fat plain yoghurt

Heat the oven to 180°C/350°F/gas 4.

Put the rice, stock, bouquet garni, seasoning and raisins in a covered dish and cook in the oven for 1 hour. Stir in the chick peas, green pepper and tomatoes, cover and cook for 15 minutes. Remove the bouquet garni and lightly fork through – the rice should be dry and flaky. Sprinkle the herbs on top. Serve the yoghurt separately.

Parsley rice

See photograph, page 62

Serves 4
Each serving: 270 kcal/1130 kJ, 6 g fibre, 2 g fat

225 g/8 oz long-grain brown rice
30 g/1 oz polyunsaturated margarine
1 large bunch spring onions, sliced
4 stalks celery, sliced

6 tbsp chopped parsley or other fresh
  herbs
seasoning

Cook the rice (see page 29).
  Meanwhile, melt the margarine in a saucepan. Add the spring onions and celery and fry gently, stirring occasionally, for 7–10 minutes or until just tender. Add the freshly cooked moist rice and chopped parsley, adjust the seasoning and allow to heat through thoroughly, stirring occasionally. Serve as an accompaniment to a main course.

Country vegetable risotto

Serves 4
Each serving: 440 kcal/1850 kJ, 23 g fibre, 1 g fat

200 g/7 oz haricot beans, soaked (see
  page 28)
15 ml/1 tbsp polyunsaturated oil
1 medium-sized onion, chopped
1 clove garlic, crushed
2 large carrots, diced
150 g/5 oz swede, diced
½ tsp celery salt
¼ tsp pepper

1 tbsp marjoram or sage
400 ml/14 fl oz stock
200 g/7 oz long-grain brown rice
200 g/7 oz fresh or frozen peas
3 tbsp chopped parsley
1 bunch spring onions, green and white
  parts, sliced
30 g/1 oz Parmesan cheese, freshly
  grated

Cook the beans (see page 28). Heat the oil in a saucepan and fry the onion and garlic for a few minutes. Add the carrots and swede and continue to cook, stirring occasionally, for 3–4 minutes. Sprinkle the seasoning, and marjoram or sage into the pan, cover with water and simmer for 20–25 minutes or until almost tender. Drain.
  Meanwhile, in another saucepan, bring the stock to the boil, sprinkle in the rice, stir and return to the boil. Lower the heat, cover the pan and cook gently for 30–35 minutes adding more stock until the rice is almost tender and the stock is absorbed. Add the beans, peas and the cooked vegetables and continue cooking for 10 minutes. Remove from the heat, adjust the seasoning, mix in half the parsley, pile on to a hot serving dish and garnish with the remaining parsley, spring onions and cheese. The consistency should be moist and creamy.
  An alternative method is to boil the beans until half-cooked, then add the vegetables and rice. As different kinds of beans and

brown rice vary in the cooking time required, the first method ensures the beans are properly cooked. The alternative cooking method, however, produces a dish with a very low fat content.

Alternatives
Many other vegetables may be used – unpeeled diced potatoes, courgettes, broad beans, green beans, leeks and so on. The texture may not be quite perfect, but the distinctive flavour of mixed fresh vegetables is very good.

Kidney bean risotto

Serves 6
Each serving: 370 kcal/1550 kJ, 11 g fibre, 7 g fat

15 ml/1 tbsp polyunsaturated oil
2 shallots or small onions, finely chopped
2 cloves garlic, crushed
1 medium-sized carrot, diced
2 courgettes, diced
2 stalks celery, diced
400 g/14 oz long-grain brown rice

1 litre/1¾ pts boiling stock
seasoning
300 g/10½ oz cooked (see page 28) or canned red kidney beans
60 g/2 oz lean bacon, grilled and diced
30 g/1 oz Parmesan cheese, grated

Heat the oil in a flameproof casserole. Add the shallots, or onions, and garlic and cook gently for 5 minutes. Stir in the carrot, courgettes and celery. Lower the heat, cover the pan and cook, stirring occasionally, for 5 minutes. Add the rice and cook, stirring occasionally, for 5 minutes. Add the boiling stock and seasoning, cover and cook gently for about 40 minutes adding more stock if required. Stir occasionally.

Add the beans and bacon and continue cooking for about 10 minutes or until the beans are hot and the rice is tender. Sprinkle the cheese over the top.

PASTA DISHES

Pasta tubes with petits pois

Serves 4
Each serving: 340 kcal/1430 kJ, 17 g fibre, 8 g fat

200 g/7 oz wholemeal pasta tubes or other small pasta shapes
500 g/18 oz fresh or frozen petits pois or garden peas
60 g/2 oz lean gammon, chopped into small cubes

1 medium-sized onion, chopped
225 g/8 oz mushrooms, thinly sliced
4 tbsp grated Parmesan cheese

Cook the pasta in boiling salted water (see page 30). Drain.

Meanwhile, put the peas, gammon and onion in a saucepan and cook in a very little water for 10 minutes. Add the mushrooms and simmer gently, stirring occasionally, for 5 minutes, or until cooked. Drain off any remaining water.

Put the cooked pasta into a hot serving dish, add the vegetables and mix together lightly. Sprinkle over the cheese and serve.

Smoked fish lasagne

Serves 6–8
6 servings Each serving: 410 kcal/1720 kJ, 8 g fibre, 9 g fat
8 servings Each serving: 310 kcal/1300 kJ, 6 g fibre, 7 g fat

300 g/10½ oz wholemeal lasagne	*4 stalks celery, chopped*
450 g/1 lb smoked haddock	*225 g/8 oz sweetcorn kernels*
1 bay leaf	
sprig of parsley	Sauce:
500 ml/18 fl oz skimmed milk	*8 tbsp wholemeal flour*
pepper	*3 tbsp polyunsaturated margarine*

Boil the lasagne in salted water until half-cooked. Drain carefully.

Heat the oven to 190°C/375°F/gas 5.

Put the haddock, bay leaf, parsley, milk and pepper in a saucepan and cook gently until the fish starts to flake. Strain the liquid and reserve for the sauce. Discard the herbs, remove any bones and skin from fish and flake.

Meanwhile, boil the celery until cooked. Drain and reserve 450 ml/¾ pint of the water for the sauce.

Mix the flaked fish, celery and corn together. Make the sauce (see page 27) using the reserved cooking liquid and celery water. Place a thin layer of the fish mixture in a non-stick dish, then a layer of lasagne, then a layer of sauce. Repeat twice, finishing with a layer of sauce.* Bake for 30–35 minutes.

*This dish can be prepared in advance to this stage, covered, and stored in the refrigerator, but allow 40–45 minutes for final cooking.

Chicken lasagne

Serves 4
Each serving: 380 kcal/1600 kJ, 9 g fibre, 13 g fat

150 g/5 oz wholemeal lasagne	*1 clove garlic, crushed*
15 ml/1 tbsp corn oil	*400 g/14 oz tomatoes*
1 large onion, chopped	*1 tbsp chopped marjoram*

4 outer stalks celery, diced and lightly
   cooked
6 tbsp chopped green pepper
170 g/6 oz cooked chicken, diced
seasoning
30 g/1 oz Parmesan cheese, grated

Country béchamel sauce:
1 small onion, chopped
small piece carrot, chopped

small piece turnip, chopped
½ bay leaf
½ blade of mace
450 ml/¾ pint skimmed milk
3 tbsp wholemeal flour
1 tbsp polyunsaturated margarine
   seasoning

Garnish:
paprika

Half-cook the lasagne in boiling salted water and drain carefully.
   Heat the oven to 190°C/375°F/gas 5.
   Heat the oil in a saucepan and cook the onion and garlic for 5 minutes or until soft. Add the tomatoes, marjoram, celery, pepper, chicken and seasoning and cook for 5 minutes.
   To make the sauce, simmer the vegetables, bay leaf and mace in nearly all the milk for 15 minutes. Remove the bay leaf and mace and mix the ingredients in a blender. Return to the pan and bring to the boil.
   Meanwhile, blend the flour with the remaining milk. Stir the hot milk mixture into the blended flour, add the margarine and seasoning, return to the pan and cook gently for a few minutes.
   Place the chicken mixture, béchamel sauce and lasagne in alternate layers in an ovenproof dish, finishing with the sauce. Scatter the cheese evenly over the top* and cook in the oven for 30–35 minutes. Sprinkle a little paprika on top and serve.

*This dish can be prepared in advance to this stage, covered and stored in the refrigerator, but allow 40–45 minutes for the final cooking.

Pasta with piquant fish sauce

Serves 4
Each serving: 340 kcal/1430 kJ, 9 g fibre, 7 g fat

15 ml/1 tbsp polyunsaturated oil
1 small onion, chopped
1 clove garlic, crushed
300 g/10½ oz canned tomatoes,
   chopped with juice
200 g/7 oz canned tuna fish in brine,
   drained and flaked

2 tbsp capers, roughly chopped
10 ml/2 tsp anchovy essence
1 tbsp finely grated orange rind
seasoning
2 tbsp chopped parsley
300 g/10½ oz wholemeal spaghetti

Heat the oil in a large saucepan. Add the onion and garlic and fry gently, stirring occasionally, for about 10 minutes. Stir in the tomatoes and simmer for a further 15 minutes. Add the tuna, capers, anchovy essence, orange rind and seasoning and bring to the simmer. Cook for 10 minutes, then stir in the parsley.

Meanwhile, cook the spaghetti in boiling salted water (see page 30). Drain well, place in a hot serving dish and pour over the sauce.

Pasta ratatouille

Serves 4
Each serving: 320 kcal/1340 kJ, 10 g fibre, 11 g fat

200 g//7 oz short-cut wholemeal macaroni
30 ml/2 tbsp corn oil
2 medium-sized onions, chopped
1 clove garlic, crushed
1 tbsp oregano
1 tbsp basil

4 medium-sized tomatoes, chopped
4 small courgettes, sliced
200 g/7 oz young broad beans
125 ml/4 fl oz chicken stock
seasoning
30 g/1 oz Parmesan cheese, grated

Heat the oven to 180°C/350°F/gas 4.

Boil the macaroni in salted water for 9–11 minutes and drain.

Meanwhile, heat the oil and cook the onion and garlic slowly until tender and golden. Stir in the herbs, tomatoes, courgettes, beans, stock and seasoning and simmer for 5 minutes. Combine the pasta and vegetables, in a baking dish, sprinkle the cheese on the top, cover and bake for 30–35 minutes.

PULSES

Dutch hot-pot

Serves 4
Each serving: 340 kcal/1430 kJ, 20 g fibre, 2 g fat

225 g/8 oz red kidney beans, soaked (see page 28)
450 g/1 lb potatoes, cubed
2 medium-sized carrots, cubed
2 medium-sized onions, sliced
150 g/5 oz cooking apple, cored and sliced

2 tbsp wholemeal flour
seasoning
70 g/2½ oz lean bacon, grilled and diced
2 tbsp frozen mixed peppers
2 tbsp chopped parsley

Lentil and split pea loaf (*top*, see page 54); Tomatoes Provençale (*bottom*, see page 42)

Put the beans and enough water to cover in a flameproof casserole. Bring to the boil and boil rapidly for 10 minutes. Lower the heat and simmer for another 20 minutes. Make up the water to about 600 ml/1 pint. Add the vegetables and apple, and cook, tightly covered, for 30–40 minutes or until the vegetables are tender but not soft.

Blend the flour with a little cold water, stir in a little of the boiling vegetable liquid, then stir into the vegetables and adjust seasoning, if necessary. Sprinkle the bacon, peppers and parsley over the top.

Although bacon is traditionally served separately, the flavour is improved when the bacon is stirred in along with chopped parsley and other favourite herbs 15 minutes before serving. Garnish with more parsley and peppers.

Tuscan beans with pasta

Serves 4
Each serving: 410 kcal/1720 kJ, 24 g fibre, 10 g fat

300 g/10½ oz haricot beans, soaked (see page 28)
30 ml/2 tbsp polyunsaturated oil
1–2 cloves garlic, crushed
2 tbsp chopped parsley
2 fresh sage leaves
200 g/7 oz canned plum tomatoes, chopped with juice
15 ml/1 tbsp tomato purée
2 medium-sized red peppers, chopped
seasoning
400 g/14 oz cooked wholemeal pasta (see page 30) in novelty shapes
2 tbsp chopped parsley

Cook the beans (see page 29). Heat the oil in a saucepan. Add the hot beans, garlic, parsley and sage and simmer gently for 5 minutes.

Meanwhile, mash together the tomatoes and tomato purée and stir them into the beans along with the red peppers and seasoning. Return to the simmer, cover and cook for 30 minutes. Spoon the bean mixture into the centre of a serving dish and arrange the pasta around the outside. Sprinkle the pasta with the parsley before serving.

Red bean flan

Serves 6
Each serving: 190 kcal/800 kJ, 6 g fibre, 6 g fat

150 ml/¼ pint skimmed milk
2 tbsp chopped parsley
¼ tsp celery salt
¼ tsp onion salt

Megadarra (*top*, see page 59) with yoghurt; Red bean flan (*bottom*)

pepper
1 egg, beaten
300 g/10½ oz canned red kidney beans or canned mixed beans
6 tbsp grated low-fat hard cheese

3 tbsp wholemeal breadcrumbs

20 cm/8 in flan case, baked blind (see page 99)

Heat the oven to 180°C/350°F/gas 4.

Add the milk, parsley, salts and pepper to the beaten egg, then add the beans. Pour into the flan case. Mix together the cheese and breadcrumbs and sprinkle over the top. Put in the oven and bake for 25–30 minutes, until firm and golden.

Lentil and split pea loaf

Serves 4   See photograph, page 51
Each serving: 300 kcal/1240 kJ, 12 g fibre, 11 g fat

100 g/3½ oz brown lentils
100 g/3½ oz split peas
6 tbsp chopped parsley
½ tsp dried mixed herbs
500 ml/18 fl oz stock or vegetable water
30 ml/2 tbsp corn oil
1 medium-sized onion, chopped

2 tbsp chopped green peppers
2 medium-sized carrots, diced
2 stalks celery, chopped
1 clove garlic, crushed
1 egg, beaten
4 tbsp natural bran flakes
60 g/2 oz minced lean cooked ham
seasoning

Put the lentils, peas, herbs and stock in a saucepan and cook until soft (see page 28) and all the liquid has been absorbed.

Heat the oven to 190°C/375°F/gas 5.

Heat the oil in a large pan and gently cook all the remaining vegetables and garlic with the lid on for 20–25 minutes, giving the pan an occasional shake or stir. The vegetables should be lightly browned. Stir into the lentil and bean mixture. Stir in the egg, bran flakes and chopped ham and season well.

Put the mixture into a greased 450 g/1 lb loaf tin or suitable baking dish, cover with foil or a lid, and bake for 40–45 minutes.

Turn out of the tin, slice and serve hot with Tomato sauce (see page 101) and any fresh vegetable. If serving cold, decorate the top with sliced radishes and thin slices of peppers, and serve with a crisp green salad.

Lentil bake

Serves 4
Each serving: 350 kcal/1470 kJ, 15 g fibre, 8 g fat

15 ml/1 tbsp corn oil
2 shallots or small onions, chopped

300 g/10½ oz red lentils
4 medium-sized tomatoes, chopped

boiling water (see method)
1 bay leaf
seasoning
½ tsp prepared mustard

60 g/2 oz Edam-type cheese, grated
3 tbsp wholemeal breadcrumbs
900 g/2 lb celery, chopped
2 tbsp chopped parsley

Heat the oil in a saucepan and gently cook the shallots or onions until they begin to soften. Add the lentils, increase the heat and cook, stirring, for 5 minutes. Stir in the tomatoes and cook over low heat for a few minutes. Just cover with boiling water, stir and continue to cook over gentle heat for about 20 minutes until all the water has been absorbed.

Heat the oven to 200°C/400°F/gas 6.

Remove the pan from the heat, mix in the bay leaf, seasoning and cheese, reserving 3 tbsp for the top. Turn into a non-stick baking dish and sprinkle the breadcrumbs and reserved cheese over the top. Bake for 30–40 minutes. Remove the bay leaf.

Meanwhile, cook the celery in a little water. Drain and turn out into a dish. Sprinkle the parsley over and serve with the lentils.

Chilli con carne

Serves 4
Each serving: 530 kcal/2230 kJ, 27 g fibre, 16 g fat

30 ml/2 tbsp corn oil
2 medium-sized onions, chopped
1 clove garlic, crushed
170 g/6 oz lean minced meat
2 tbsp wholemeal flour
22 ml/1½ tbsp tomato purée
250 ml/9 fl oz stock, hot
1–3 tsp chilli powder

2–3 drops Tabasco sauce (optional)
400 g/14 oz canned tomatoes, chopped
*   with juice*
450 g/1 lb red kidney beans, soaked
*   (see page 28)*
salt
1 medium–large green pepper, chopped

Heat the oil in a sauté pan and gently fry the onions and garlic for 5 minutes. Toss the meat in the flour, add to the pan and cook, stirring, until brown. Mix the tomato purée with the hot stock and gradually stir into the pan. Add the chilli powder, Tabasco sauce, if using, tomatoes and beans and boil for 10 minutes. Stir, cover tightly and simmer gently for 1–1¼ hours or until the beans are cooked. Ten minutes before serving, stir in salt to taste and the green pepper.

Alternatives
Use a mixture of meat and textured vegetable protein (TVP) in place of all meat.

Instead of red kidney beans use other dried beans. The cooking time should be adjusted (see respective cooking times on page 28).

Pease pudding

Serves 4
Each serving: 230 kcal/970 kJ, 11 g fibre, 5 g fat

225 g/8 oz whole dried peas, soaked
(see page 28)
1 large Spanish onion, sliced
1 litre/1¾ pints water
seasoning

pinch grated nutmeg
1 egg, lightly beaten
15 ml/1 tbsp polyunsaturated
margarine
6 tbsp wholemeal breadcrumbs

Heat the oven to 190°C/357°F/gas 5.

Put the peas, onion and water in a saucepan and cook until soft (see page 28). Drain off any excess liquid and blend to a purée. Season well with salt, pepper and freshly grated nutmeg, and beat in the egg.

Grease a small non-stick baking dish with the margarine, sprinkle thickly with breadcrumbs and spoon in the pea mixture. Sprinkle any remaining breadcrumbs over the top. Bake for 30 minutes, then remove from the oven and set aside for 10 minutes to allow the pudding to shrink. Turn out and serve.

Alternatively, steam the mixture in a pudding basin or in individual moulds covered with foil. Other flavourings, such as 3–4 cloves or a bay leaf can be added to the cooking water, or fresh herbs such as marjoram can be added to the peas in the blender.

Serve with boiled lean ham or bacon. Or serve as a snack with Tomato or Barbecue sauce (see pages 101–2), or with a salad of green pepper rings, onion and sliced tomatoes or any of the other salads (see pages 36–40).

Vegetarian bean paella

Serves 4
Each serving: 420 kcal/1770 kJ, 20 g fibre, 10 g fat

100 g/3½ oz red kidney beans, soaked
(see page 28)
60 g/2 oz mung beans, soaked (see page 28)
225 g/8 oz long-grain brown rice
450 ml/¾ pint water
½ tsp powdered saffron
salt
1 small aubergine, diced
30 ml/2 tbsp corn oil

1 Spanish onion, chopped
1 clove garlic, crushed
1 stalk celery, chopped
1 medium–large green pepper, chopped
2 large carrots, diced
300 g/10½ oz canned tomatoes, drained
115 g/4 oz fresh button mushrooms
2 tbsp chopped parsley

Cook the beans (see page 28). Meanwhile, put the rice, water, saffron and 1 tsp salt in a saucepan and cook for 30 minutes (see page 29). Sprinkle salt over the aubergine, leave for 20 minutes, then wipe dry.

Heat the oil in another saucepan and gently cook the onion and garlic for 5 minutes. Add the aubergine, celery, green pepper and carrots and cook gently, stirring occasionally, for 10 minutes. Stir in the tomatoes and mushrooms and continue cooking for 5 minutes. Gently mix the vegetables and beans into the rice, adjust the seasoning if necessary. Cover the pan and continue cooking gently for 15 minutes. Turn off the heat and keep the mixture warm for 10 minutes. Gently fork in the parsley and serve.

Haricot bean and vegetable casserole

Serves 4
Each serving: 300 kcal/1240 kJ, 24 g fibre, 5 g fat

300 g/10½ oz haricot beans, soaked (see page 28)
15 ml/1 tbsp corn oil
1 large onion, finely chopped
1 clove garlic, crushed
2 outer stalks celery, finely chopped
2 medium-sized green peppers, sliced
2 medium-sized carrots, sliced
45 ml/3 tbsp tomato purée
1 tbsp oregano
4 tbsp chopped parsley
seasoning
250 ml/9 fl oz strong stock, hot
6 medium-sized tomatoes, halved

Cook the beans (see page 28). Heat the oil in a flameproof casserole and gently cook the onion and garlic until golden brown. Stir in the celery, green peppers, carrots and beans and cook over low heat for 10 minutes. Add the tomato purée, herbs, seasoning and stock. Cover and cook gently for 30 minutes. Place the tomatoes, cut side up, on top of the ingredients and continue cooking for 15 minutes.

For variety, other types of beans may be used.

Chick pea and leek quiche

Serves 6
Each serving: 310 kcal/1300 kJ, 8 g fibre, 10 g fat

Pastry:
200 g/7 oz wholemeal flour
1½ tsp baking powder
¼ tsp garlic salt
¼ tsp celery salt
¼ tsp dry mustard
70 g/2½ oz low-fat margarine spread
100 g/3½ oz mashed potatoes

Filling:
250 ml/9 fl oz skimmed milk

4 young leeks, sliced
1 clove garlic, crushed
2 small eggs
100 g/3½ oz skimmed-milk cheese
1 tsp onion salt
pepper
250 g/9 oz cooked chick peas (see page 29)
small bunch spring onions, chopped
30 g/1 oz Parmesan cheese, grated

Heat the oven to 200°C/400°F/gas 6.

To make the pastry, mix the flour with the baking powder, salts and mustard and rub in the margarine until the mixture resembles fine breadcrumbs. Knead in the mashed potato until a ball of stiff dough is formed. Roll to the required size between sheets of polythene or greaseproof paper. Peel off the top layer of paper. Lift the dough on the bottom layer of paper and invert to line a 20–25 cm/9–10 inch flan dish. Prick the bottom of the pastry and bake for 15 minutes. Remove from the oven and reset the heat to 180°C/350°F/gas 4.

Meanwhile, put the milk, leeks and garlic in a saucepan and simmer for 5 minutes. Put the eggs, cheese and seasonings in a bowl and beat well. Stir in the chick peas, leeks and milk. Pour the mixture into the flan case, sprinkle the top with the spring onions and then the cheese. Bake for 50–55 minutes or until the filling is set. Serve hot or cold.

Bean pie

Serves 4
Each serving: 390 kcal/1640 kJ, 25 g fibre, 2 g fat

200 g/7 oz haricot or other beans, soaked (see page 28)
100 g/3½ oz black-eyed or other fairly small beans, soaked (see page 28)
2 medium-sized onions, chopped
2 medium-sized peppers, chopped
150 g/5 oz mushrooms, sliced
400 g/14 oz canned tomatoes, chopped with juice

1 tbsp oregano or fresh mixed herbs seasoning
chicken stock, as required

Topping:
500 g/18 oz mashed potatoes
60 ml/4 tbsp skimmed milk mixed with 60 g/2 oz low-fat hard cheese, grated

Heat the oven to 200°C/400°F/gas 6.

Put the beans in a saucepan, cover with water and bring to the boil. Lower the heat, cover the pan and simmer for 45 minutes.

Layer the beans and vegetables, except the mashed potatoes, in a strong stoneware pot or casserole, sprinkling a little seasoning and herbs between the layers. Add sufficient stock to come about level with the bean mixture. Cover with the mashed potatoes and sprinkle with the cheese.

Put the casserole in the oven and bake for 40–45 minutes until brown.

Hot Mexican beans

Serves 4
Each serving: 210 kcal/880 kJ, 16 g fibre, 5 g fat

15 ml/1 tbsp corn oil

225 g/8 oz speckled Mexican beans,

soaked (see page 28)
2 medium-sized onions, chopped
1 clove garlic, crushed
6 medium-sized tomatoes, chopped

¼ tsp chilli powder
few drops Tabasco sauce
1½ tbsp chopped oregano
seasoning

Cook the beans (see page 28). Heat the oil in a saucepan and cook the onion and garlic gently for 10 minutes. Stir in the onions, garlic, tomatoes, chilli powder, Tabasco, oregano and seasoning and bring to simmering point. Stir in the beans and simmer, covered, for 20 minutes.

Megadarra
See photograph, page 52

Serves 4
Each serving: 480 kcal/2020 kJ, 12 g fibre, 9 g fat

300 g/10½ oz Continental brown
  lentils, soaked (see page 28)
450 ml/¾ pint water
3 medium-sized onions (1 chopped and
  2 halved and thinly sliced)
30 ml/2 tbsp polyunsaturated oil

150 g/5 oz long-grain brown rice
1 tsp ground cumin (optional)
½ tsp ground coriander (optional)
seasoning
1 clove garlic, crushed (optional)
300 ml/½ pint low-fat plain yoghurt

Put the lentils and water in a flameproof casserole and bring to the boil. Lower the heat, half cover the pan and simmer gently for 15 minutes.

Meanwhile, fry the chopped onion in a little oil until golden brown. Stir the fried onions, rice, spices, if using, and seasoning into the lentils. Return to the simmer, cover and cook gently for about 45 minutes, or until cooked. If the mixture becomes too dry, add a little more water or, if the water is not all absorbed, finish off without a lid for a few minutes. Adjust the seasoning if necessary.

Heat the remaining oil in a small frying pan and fry the sliced onions with the garlic, if used, until dark brown, almost burnt. Spoon the lentil and rice mixture into a shallow dish. Sprinkle the browned onions over the top and serve with the yoghurt in a separate bowl.

FISH, POULTRY AND MEAT

FISH DISHES

Spanish baked fish

Serves 4
Each serving: 140 kcal/590 kJ, 2 g fibre, 2 g fat

5 ml/1 tsp corn oil
1 Spanish onion, chopped
*400 g/14 oz canned tomatoes, chopped
  with juice*
seasoning
1½ tsp dried marjoram
*1 small can (or ½ a fresh) red
  peppers, chopped*

*125 ml/4 fl oz dry white wine or
  cider*
2 tsp cornflour
15 ml/1 tbsp water
6 green olives, stoned and sliced
1 tbsp capers
1 tbsp chopped parsley
400 g/14 oz white fish fillets

Heat the oil and cook the onion slowly until soft. Add the tomatoes, seasoning, marjoram, pepper and wine, or cider. Cover and simmer 20 minutes.

Heat the oven to 200°C/400°F/gas 6.

Blend the cornflour with the water, stir into the sauce and simmer for 2 minutes. Add half the olives, capers and parsley. Place the fish in a non-stick baking dish and pour the sauce over. Bake for 20–25 minutes or until the fish flakes easily, basting with the sauce after 10 minutes and immediately prior to serving. Serve decorated with the remaining olives, capers and parsley.

Rolled stuffed fillets of fish

Serves 4
Each serving: 150 kcal/620 kJ, 2 g fibre, 6 g fat

250 g/9 oz frozen mixed vegetables
90 ml/6 tbsp fish stock
*400 g/14 oz white fish fillets, skinned
  (4 fillets)*

2 tsp polyunsaturated margarine
lemon slices
sprigs of parsley

Rolled stuffed fish
Overleaf: Quick chicken charlotte (*left*, see page 67); Sweet and sour veal with parsley rice (*top right*, see pages 69 and 46); Rissoles (*bottom right*, see page 71)

Stuffing

30 g/1 oz wholemeal breadcrumbs *pinch dried mixed herbs*
2 tbsp chopped spring onion *seasoning*
1 tsp grated lemon rind *2 tbsp skimmed milk curd cheese*

Heat the oven to 180°C/350°F/gas 4.

Put the vegetables into a non-stick baking dish and pour over the stock.

To make the stuffing, mix all the ingredients together and, using a fork, work in the cheese. Spread the stuffing on the skinned side of the fish fillets and roll up, starting at the tail end. Place on top of the vegetables in the baking dish and dot each fillet with a little margarine.

Cover the dish and bake for 25–30 minutes, or until the fish is cooked. Serve straight from the dish, garnished with lemon slices and parsley.

Salmon kedgeree

Serves 4
Each serving: 280 kcal/1180 kJ, 3 g fibre, 6 g fat

200 g/7 oz long-grain brown rice *seasoning*
½–1 tsp curry powder *1 hard-boiled egg, yolk and white*
200 g/7 oz canned salmon*, drained, *chopped separately*
skinned and flaked *2 tbsp chopped parsley*

Cook the rice (see page 29). Sprinkle the curry powder over the rice. Add the fish and a little seasoning and mix in gently with a fork. Cook over low heat until hot. Pile into a heated dish and garnish with the egg yolk and white, and parsley.

*Left-over cooked fresh salmon or other similar fish may be substituted for the canned salmon.

Fish pie

Serves 4–6
4 servings   Each serving: 390 kcal/1640 kJ, 19 g fibre, 3 g fat
6 servings   Each serving: 260 kcal/1090 kJ, 12 g fibre, 2 g fat

200 g/7 oz haricot beans, soaked (see *(reconstituted volume if condensed*
page 28) *soup used)*
200 g/7 oz cooked white fish, flaked *4 medium-sized tomatoes, thinly sliced*
15 ml/1 tbsp lemon juice
2 tbsp chopped parsley Topping:
225 g/8 oz canned mixed vegetables* *90 ml/6 tbsp skimmed milk*
275 ml/10 fl oz canned asparagus soup *680 g/1½ lb hot mashed potato*

Sweetcorn, rice and pepper salad (*top*, see page 39); Mackerel mousse (*bottom*, see page 66)

Cook the beans (see page 28), then lightly mash with a fork. Mix with the fish, lemon juice, parsley and mixed vegetables. Heat the soup in a saucepan, stir in the bean and fish mixture and heat through for 5–10 minutes, then turn into a hot pie dish and cover with the sliced tomatoes. Mix 60 ml/4 tbsp of the milk into the potato and spread over the tomatoes. Brush the remaining milk over the potato and brown under a hot grill.

Alternatively, the pie can be prepared in advance, cooled, kept in the refrigerator, then cooked in a moderately hot oven (190°C/375°F/gas 5) for 25–30 minutes.

*Calculated as equal amounts of carrots, corn kernels, peas and broad beans.

Mackerel mousse   See photograph, page 64

Serves 4
Each serving: 90 kcal/380 kJ, negligible fibre, 4 g fat

200 g/7 oz canned mackerel fillets,   *seasoning*
    drained and boned   *3 tsp gelatine dissolved in 45 ml/3 tbsp*
200 ml/⅓ pint tomato juice   *hot water*
5 ml/1 tsp wine vinegar   *3–4 small gherkins, chopped*
2–3 drops Tabasco sauce   *lemon slices*
2–3 drops Worcester sauce   *chopped parsley*

Place the mackerel, tomato juice, vinegar, Tabasco sauce and Worcester sauce in a blender and process to a purée. Adjust the seasoning. Stir in the dissolved gelatine and fold in the gherkins.

Pour the mixture into a 600 ml/1 pint soufflé or other suitable dish and leave in the refrigerator until set. Garnish with lemon slices and parsley before serving. Serve with a high-fibre salad (see pages 36–40). Alternatively, omit the gelatine and serve as a pâté with toast.

Mackerel croquettes

Serves 4
Each serving: 170 kcal/710 kJ, 3 g fibre, 5 g fat

150 g/5 oz smoked mackerel, cooked   *½ tsp lemon juice or vinegar, or to*
    and flaked   *taste*
150 g/5 oz bean curd (tofu), drained
150 g/5 oz freshly mashed potato   Coating
2 tbsp chopped parsley   *5 tbsp wholemeal breadcrumbs*
1 tsp chopped tarragon   *5 tbsp rolled oats*
½ tsp onion salt   *1 egg, beaten*
pepper

Heat the oven to 220°C/425°F/gas 7.

Mix all the ingredients together in a bowl. Roll into a long cylinder and cut into 8 croquettes.

To coat, mix the breadcrumbs and the oats together in a polythene bag. One at a time, dip the croquettes into the egg, then shake gently in the bag, pressing the mixture firmly into the croquettes. Put the croquettes in the refrigerator to firm up for 30 minutes before cooking.

Place the croquettes on a non-stick tray or baking sheet and bake in the oven for 15–20 minutes until golden brown. Alternatively, cook under a medium grill.

Serve with home-made Tomato sauce (see page 101) or tomatoes baked at the same time as the fish.

POULTRY DISHES

Quick chicken charlotte

Serves 4   See photograph, page 62
Each serving: 370 kcal/1570 kJ, 7 g fibre, 12 g fat

100 g/3½ oz wholemeal breadcrumbs
100 g/3½ oz rolled oats
340 g/12 oz cooked chicken, neatly diced
mixed vegetables, fresh, canned or frozen, chopped e.g: 60 g/2 oz each celery, carrots, turnip, peas, broad beans, sweetcorn kernels
1 tbsp mixed herbs
seasoning
300 g/10½ oz canned mushroom soup (reconstituted volume if condensed soup used)
150 ml/¼ pint water

Heat the oven to 200°C/400°F/gas 6.

Mix the breadcrumbs and the oats together. Grease a baking dish and sprinkle the base with one-third of the mixture. Mix together the chicken, vegetables, herbs and seasoning. Spoon into the baking dish and pour in the soup and water. Cover with the remaining crumbs-and-oat mixture and bake for 45 minutes.

Chicken curry

Serves 4
Each serving: 260 kcal/1090 kJ, 8 g fibre, 7 g fat

1 tbsp polyunsaturated margarine
1 medium-sized onion, chopped
1 medium-sized eating apple, chopped
1 tbsp curry powder, or to taste
1 tsp curry paste
2 tbsp wholemeal flour
450 ml/¾ pint chicken stock
10 ml/2 tsp lemon juice
½ tsp salt
1 tbsp mango chutney
3 tbsp sultanas
150 ml/¼ pint low-fat plain yoghurt
200 g/7 oz cooked mung or other beans
200 g/7 oz cooked chicken, diced

Heat the margarine in a non-stick saucepan and fry the onion and apple until softened. Add the curry powder and curry paste and cook gently, stirring, for 10 minutes. Stir in the flour and cook for a few minutes. Gradually stir in the stock and bring to the boil. Add the lemon juice, salt, chutney and sultanas. Finally, stir in the yoghurt, beans and chicken and heat through.

Serve with plainly cooked brown rice (see page 29).

Chicken casserole

Serves 4
Each serving: 210 kcal/880 kJ, 6 g fibre, 7 g fat

1 tbsp polyunsaturated margarine
300 ml/½ pint chicken stock
4 small chicken portions (450 g/1 lb total), skinned
2 medium-sized onions, chopped
2 medium-sized carrots, sliced

seasoning
sprig of rosemary or tarragon
2 green peppers, chopped
200 g/7 oz cooked haricot beans (see page 28) or other cooked beans
2 tbsp wholemeal flour

Heat the oven to 190°C/375°F/gas 5.

Heat the oil with a few spoonfuls of stock in a large flameproof casserole and fry the chicken portions until pale golden brown. Remove from the pan and set aside on a plate. Add the onions to the pan and cook gently, stirring occasionally, for 5 minutes. Return the chicken pieces to the pan with the remaining stock, carrots, seasoning and herbs. Cover the casserole and cook in the oven for 30 minutes.

Mix the peppers and beans into the casserole and return to the oven for a further 30 minutes or until all the vegetables are cooked.

Blend the flour with a little cold water, stir into the casserole and cook for 5 minutes until thickened. Adjust the seasoning and serve.

Moroccan chicken

Serves 6
Each serving: 300 kcal/1260 kJ, 11 g fibre, 10 g fat

1 tbsp polyunsaturated margarine
100 ml/3½ fl oz chicken stock
1 small chicken (about 1 kg/2¼ lb) or chicken joints, skinned
400 g/14 oz canned tomatoes, chopped with juice
1 dozen shallots or small onions

1 lemon, quartered
2 cloves garlic, crushed
bouquet garni
seasoning
400 g/14 oz canned chick peas
250 g/9 oz small or sliced mushrooms
12 green olives, stoned and halved

Heat the margarine and a few spoonfuls of stock in a large flame-proof casserole and fry the chicken, turning it to brown all over. Add the tomatoes, shallots or onions, lemon, garlic, bouquet garni, seasoning and the remainder of the stock. Bring to the boil, cover and simmer slowly for 1 hour. Top up with a little more stock if necessary.

Add the chick peas and mushrooms and simmer for a further 30 minutes or until the chicken is very tender and breaking away from the bone and the peas have started to break down. Remove and discard the lemon, bouquet garni and the chicken bones. Adjust the seasoning, if necessary, and scatter the olives over the top. Serve in the casserole accompanied by plainly cooked brown rice.

An alternative way to serve is to add the cooked rice to the casserole before garnishing with the olives.

MEAT DISHES

Veal goulash

Serves 4
Each serving: 230 kcal/970 kJ, 8 g fibre, 6 g fat

1 tbsp polyunsaturated margarine	*1 tbsp oregano*
300 ml/½ pint chicken or veal stock	*seasoning*
2 medium-sized onions, chopped	*250 g/9 oz canned red kidney beans*
250 g/9 oz lean pie veal, cubed	*115 g/4 oz mushrooms, sliced*
1 clove garlic, crushed	*3 medium-sized red peppers, sliced*
4 tsp paprika	*2 tbsp wholemeal flour*
400 g/14 oz canned tomatoes	*150 ml/¼ pint low-fat plain yoghurt*

Heat the margarine with a few spoonfuls of stock in a non-stick casserole and fry the onions until golden brown. Draw the onions to one side of the casserole and fry the meat until browned. Add the remaining stock, garlic, paprika, tomatoes, oregano and seasoning. Cover the casserole and cook gently for 1½ hours.

Add the beans, mushrooms and peppers to the casserole and continue to cook for about 15 minutes or until all the ingredients are cooked.

Blend the flour with a little water and stir it in. Bring the goulash to the boil and cook, stirring, for about 3 minutes. Stir in the yoghurt and serve from the casserole.

Sweet and sour veal   See photograph, page 62

Serves 4
Each serving: 240 kcal/1010 kJ, 12 g fibre, 2 g fat

300 g/10½ oz lean pie veal, cubed   *1 small onion, chopped*

1 medium-sized carrot, diced
3 stalks celery, sliced
4 tbsp frozen diced peppers
150 g/5 oz mung beans, soaked (see page 28)
15 ml/1 tbsp soy sauce, or to taste
30 ml/2 tbsp red wine vinegar

300 g/10½ oz canned pineapple in natural juice, drained and cut into chunks; reserve juice
1 tsp ground ginger
300 ml/½ pint veal or chicken stock
seasoning
2 tbsp wholemeal flour

Put the veal, vegetables and beans in a non-stick casserole. Stir the soy sauce, vinegar, pineapple juice and ginger into the stock, and pour over the veal and vegetables. Cover and simmer for about 1 hour or until the meat is tender.

Add the pineapple chunks and seasoning and return to the simmer for 5 minutes. Mix the flour with a little cold water, add to the casserole, bring to boiling point and cook, stirring, for about 3 minutes. Serve with boiled long-grain brown rice or wholegrain pasta noodles.

Other lean meats such as chicken, turkey, rabbit or pigeon cut in small pieces may be substituted for the veal.

Beef and black bean casserole

Serves 4
Each serving: 390 kcal/1640 kJ, 26 g fibre, 8 g fat

300 g/10½ oz black beans, soaked (see page 28)
15 ml/1 tbsp polyunsaturated oil
225 g/8 oz lean beef, diced
2 medium-sized leeks, thinly sliced
1 clove garlic, crushed
300 ml/½ pint beef stock
2 stalks celery, sliced
2 medium-sized carrots, sliced

15 ml/1 tbsp tomato purée
450 g/1 lb canned tomatoes, chopped with juice
1 bay leaf
1 tsp dried oregano
seasoning
2 tbsp wholemeal flour
2 tbsp chopped chives

Cook the beans (see page 28). Meanwhile, heat the oil in a flame-proof casserole and add the meat. Fry gently, stirring, until lightly browned. Remove the meat with a slotted spoon and set aside on a plate.

Add the leeks, garlic and a few spoonfuls of stock to the pan. Stir well, reduce the heat to low, cover the pan and cook for 10–15 minutes, or until the leeks are tender. Return the meat to the pan with the remaining stock, celery, carrots, tomato purée, tomatoes, herbs and seasoning and bring to the boil. Lower the heat, cover the pan and simmer for 45 minutes.

Add the beans and simmer for a further 30–45 minutes or until the meat is tender and the beans soft and have absorbed the mixed vegetable flavours.

Blend the flour with a little cold water, stir into the casserole and return to the boil. Cook gently for a further 5 minutes or until thickened. Sprinkle with chives and serve straight from the casserole.

Rissoles
See photograph, page 62

Serves 4
Each serving: 280 kcal/1180 kJ, 15 g fibre, 5 g fat

225 g/8 oz lean cooked meat
200 g/7 oz cooked haricot beans (see page 28)
small bunch of spring onions (6–7), chopped
60 g/2 oz wholemeal bread
2 tbsp chopped parsley
seasoning
1–2 tsp Worcester sauce
1 egg, lightly beaten

Heat the oven to 220°C/425°F/gas 7.

Mince the meat, beans, spring onions and bread together. Mix with all the remaining ingredients and form into 8 flat rissoles about 12 mm/½ inch thick.

Place the rissoles on a non-stick ovenproof dish or baking sheet and bake in the oven for 20–25 minutes. Alternatively, brown quickly under a hot grill, reduce the heat and grill more slowly for 10–15 minutes.

Serve with gravy or Tomato sauce (see page 101).

Cottage pie

Serves 4
Each serving: 440 kcal/1840 kJ, 18 g fibre, 6 g fat

200 g/7 oz haricot beans, soaked (see page 28)
300 g/10½ oz canned tomato soup (reconstituted volume if condensed)
1 Spanish onion, finely chopped
1 medium-sized red pepper, finely chopped
60 g/2 oz slice wholemeal bread, crumbled
200 g/7 oz cooked lean meat, minced
4 tbsp chopped parsley
seasoning
450 g/1 lb potatoes, cubed
60 g/2 oz red lentils
pinch nutmeg
30 ml/2 tbsp skimmed milk

Cook the beans (see page 28). Mix the soup, onion and pepper in a saucepan and simmer gently for 10 minutes. Add the bread and stir and mash with a wooden spoon until the ingredients are well mixed. Stir in the meat and beans, bring to the boil and heat through thoroughly, stirring occasionally. Mix in the parsley and seasoning. Transfer to a pie dish.

Meanwhile, cook the potatoes and lentils together. Mash with the nutmeg and a little salt. Spread the mixture over the pie to cover. Brush with the milk,* brown lightly under the grill and serve.

*The pie can be made to this stage, left to cool, covered and refrigerated. Bake in a moderately hot oven for 25–30 minutes when required.

Hot-pot with mixed vegetables

Serves 4
Each serving: 300 kcal/1260 kJ, 13 g fibre, 3 g fat

200 g/7 oz cooked lean meat, diced
1 medium-sized carrot, thinly sliced
4 young leeks, thinly sliced
100 g/3½ oz cauliflower, broken into
* small sprigs*
3 stalks celery, sliced
400 g/14 oz canned kidney beans
* (without sugar) or cooked beans (see*
* page 28)*

sprig of thyme or ¼ tsp dried mixed
* herbs*
seasoning
3 medium-sized tomatoes, sliced
meat stock or gravy
1 tbsp chopped chives

Heat the oven to 170°C/325°F/gas 3.
  Place the meat, vegetables (except the tomatoes) and beans in layers in a large casserole, sprinkling herbs and seasoning between the layers. Top with a layer of tomatoes, arranged in an over-lapping pattern. Add enough stock or gravy almost to reach the tomatoes. Bake, covered in the oven for 45–50 minutes.
  Sprinkle the chives on top and serve straight from the casserole.

Beef and bean goulash

Serves 4
Each serving: 330 kcal/1390 kJ, 16 g fibre, 8 g fat

15 ml/1 tbsp corn oil
2 large onions, chopped
300 ml/½ pint meat stock
1 clove garlic, crushed
4 tsp paprika
200 g/7 oz lean stewing steak, cut in
* neat pieces*
3 tbsp wholemeal flour

400 g/14 oz canned tomatoes, chopped
* in juice*
1 tbsp marjoram
200 g/7 oz red kidney beans, soaked
* (see page 28)*
3 medium-sized red peppers, sliced
seasoning
150 ml/¼ pint low-fat plain yoghurt

Heat the oil in a flameproof casserole and add the onions with a few tbsp stock. Cook, stirring, for about 5 minutes, until the onions begin to soften and brown slightly. Stir in the garlic and paprika, then stir in the meat. Sprinkle on the flour, stir in the tomatoes, marjoram and remaining stock and simmer, covered, for 1 hour.

Hot-pot with mixed vegetables

Add the beans and cook for about 45 minutes. Add the peppers and salt and cook for about 15 minutes until the meat and beans are tender. Serve with the yoghurt spooned over.

Ragoût of lamb

Serves 4
Each serving: 280 kcal/1180 kJ, 14 g fibre, 9 g fat

15 ml/1 tbsp polyunsaturated oil
225 g/8 oz lean lamb, diced
1 medium-sized leek, sliced
400 g/14 oz canned tomatoes, chopped with juice
1 tsp paprika
salt
400 g/14 oz canned haricot or other beans or cooked beans (see page 28)
4 tbsp chopped parsley
1 tbsp wholemeal flour
1 large bunch spring onions, chopped
150 ml/¼ pint low-fat plain yoghurt

Heat the oil in a flameproof casserole. Add the meat and fry gently, stirring, until lightly browned. Add the leek, tomatoes, paprika and salt and bring to the boil. Cover the casserole, lower the heat and simmer for 1 hour.

Add the beans and parsley and simmer for 30 minutes, or until the meat is tender.

Blend the flour with a little cold water, and stir into the casserole along with the spring onions. Cook for a further 5 minutes or until thickened. Stir in the yoghurt just before serving.

ENTERTAINING

Mushroom soup

Serves 4
Each serving: 110 kcal/460 kJ, 5 g fibre, 1 g fat

15 g/½ oz polyunsaturated margarine
600 ml/1 pint white stock
1 medium-sized onion, sliced
450 g/1 lb mushrooms, sliced
300 ml/½ pint skimmed milk
good pinch ground mace or grated nutmeg
sprigs of parsley
½ tsp salt
pepper
juice of 1 lemon
60 g/2 oz sliced wholemeal bread, toasted
paprika
chopped parsley

Salmon mousse with cucumber (see page 77)

Melt the margarine with a few spoonfuls of the stock in a saucepan. Add the onion and cook gently, stirring, for about 5 minutes. Add the mushrooms and continue cooking for a further 5 minutes. Stir in the remaining stock, milk, mace or nutmeg, parsley sprigs and seasoning. Cover the pan and simmer gently for about 30 minutes.

Purée the soup in a blender, return to the rinsed saucepan and reheat gently. When hot, remove from the heat, stir in the lemon juice and adjust the seasoning.

Dice the toast into croutons and serve with the soup. Sprinkle a little paprika and chopped parsley over the soup before serving.

Gazpacho

Serves 4
Each serving: 50 kcal/210 kJ, 2 g fibre, negligible fat

450 g/1 lb ripe tomatoes
1 small onion
1 small green pepper
½ cucumber
1 clove garlic, crushed
150 ml/¼ pint chicken stock

340 ml/12 fl oz tomato juice
30 ml/2 tbsp cider vinegar
30 ml/2 tbsp dry red wine
celery salt
pepper

Chop the vegetables coarsely, reserving a little cucumber for decoration. Place all the ingredients in a blender and purée until smooth but leave a few small pieces of vegetable visible. Taste for seasoning and adjust, if necessary. Keep in the refrigerator until required. Serve in chilled soup bowls, garnished with diced cucumber.

Cock-a-leekie soup

Serves 4, twice
Each serving: 160 kcal/670 kJ, 3 g fibre, 4 g fat

3 cloves
6 peppercorns
1½ kg/3 lb small boiling chicken, trussed*
2 litres/3½ pints beef or veal stock

8 young leeks
salt
4 tbsp brown rice
4 tbsp chopped parsley

Tie the cloves and peppercorns in a muslin bag and put in a large saucepan with the chicken, stock, 2 leeks and salt. Bring to the boil, skimming off any scum. Lower the heat, cover the pan and simmer, skimming the surface occasionally, for about 3 hours or until the chicken is tender.

Remove the chicken and muslin bag from the pan and add the

remaining leeks and the rice. Simmer, covered, for about 40 minutes or until the rice is cooked.

Meanwhile, remove the chicken flesh from the carcass and chop finely. Add the chicken to the pan with the parsley, adjust the seasoning and serve.

*Chicken pieces may be used. Adjust cooking times.

Chicken and tarragon pâté with walnuts

See photograph, page 84

Each 30 g/1 oz: 40 kcal/170 kJ, 1 g fibre, 2 g fat

300 g/10½ oz cooked chicken
200 g/7 oz bean curd (tofu), drained
30 ml/2 tbsp proprietary low-calorie
  salad cream
10 ml/2 tsp lemon juice, or to taste
1 tbsp finely chopped tarragon
1 tbsp finely chopped chives (optional)

seasoning

Garnish
2 tbsp walnut pieces
sprigs of fresh tarragon
lemon wedges

Mince the chicken finely. Add the remaining ingredients and beat until smooth. Put into a mould or serving dish and garnish with a few walnut pieces and sprigs of tarragon. Keep in the refrigerator until required. Serve accompanied by lemon wedges and a salad.

For special occasions, press into 8 small pots, decorate each with tarragon leaves and a small piece of walnut, then spoon a little aspic jelly on top. Allow the jelly to set in the refrigerator and serve.

Note: Other varieties of herbs may be substituted for the tarragon. Try a mixture of dill, spring onions and parsley.

Salmon mousse with cucumber

Serves 6   See photograph, page 74

Each serving: 120 kcal/520 kJ, negligible fibre, 5 g fat

300 g/10½ oz canned pink salmon,
  drained and boned
150 ml/¼ pint skimmed milk
150 ml/¼ pint low-fat plain yoghurt
30 ml/2 tbsp lemon juice
15 ml/1 tbsp tomato purée

4 tsp gelatine dissolved in 60 ml/
  4 tbsp hot water
few drops red food colouring (optional)
seasoning
1 egg, separated
thinly sliced cucumber, (with skin),
  marinated in wine vinegar

Purée all the ingredients except the egg white and cucumber in a blender.

Whisk the egg white until stiff and fold into the mixture. Pour into a mould or individual moulds, cover and leave in the refrigerator until set.

Unmould and decorate with the cucumber slices. Serve with Potato salad (see page 40).

Sea bass, Dugléré style

Serves 4
Each serving: 250 kcal/1050 kJ, 4 g fibre, 4 g fat

1 sea bass*, weighing about 1 kg/2¼ lb
1 tbsp finely chopped onion
4 medium-sized tomatoes, chopped
100 g/3½ oz canned sweetcorn kernels
100 g/3½ oz green beans, sliced
1 tbsp chopped parsley
sprig of thyme
½ bay leaf

small clove garlic, crushed
seasoning
300 ml/½ pint dry white wine or cider
4 tsp low-fat margarine spread
1 tbsp soya bean flour (defatted)

Garnish
1 tbsp chopped parsley
lemon wedges

Heat the oven to 180°C/350°F/gas 4.

Have the fish cleaned, scaled and boned at the fishmongers. The fish head should be removed and the fish folded back to its original shape. Put the whole fish in a non-stick baking dish and cut across in 8 even-sized slices.

Mix together the vegetables, herbs, garlic and seasoning and put around the fish. Pour the wine or cider over, dot with the margarine, cover and bake for 30–40 minutes. When cooked, remove the pieces of fish with a slotted spoon and arrange in a fish shape on a long serving dish. Remove the thyme and bay leaf from the cooked vegetables, put the vegetables around the fish and keep hot.

Blend the flour with a little water, stir into the liquid in the baking dish and cook, stirring, until the sauce thickens. Pour over the fish, sprinkle with parsley and serve with lemon wedges.

*Other fish may be used instead of sea bass.

Plaice piquant

Serves 4
Each serving: 220 kcal/920 kJ, 8 g fibre, 7 g fat

15 ml/1 tbsp lemon juice
1 small onion, finely chopped
4 courgettes, cut in small sticks
150 g/5 oz frozen peas
60 g/2 oz canned anchovy fillets, drained

1 tbsp capers
4 tbsp chopped parsley
seasoning
500 g/18 oz plaice fillets (4 fillets)
4 tsp low-fat margarine spread
lemon wedges

Heat the oven to 180°C/350°F/gas 4.

Mix the onion, courgettes and peas with anchovy fillets, capers, half the parsley and seasoning. Place the vegetable mixture in a saucepan with a little stock, cover and half cook.

Put the plaice in a large flat non-stick baking dish and sprinkle with the lemon juice. Pile the vegetable mixture on top of the fish. Dot with the margarine, cover and bake for 20–25 minutes, or until all is cooked.

Sprinkle the remainder of the parsley on top. Serve with lemon wedges.

Creole baked fish

Serves 4
Each serving: 260 kcal/1090 kJ, 5 g fibre, 1 g fat

500 g/18 oz thick white fish fillets (4 fillets)
400 g/14 oz canned tomatoes, drained and chopped, juice reserved
2 medium-sized onions, finely chopped
1 green pepper, chopped
150 g/5 oz cooked black-eyed beans (see page 28)

1 clove garlic, crushed
small sprig of thyme
small piece of cinnamon
seasoning

Garnish
2 tbsp chopped parsley
lemon wedges

Heat the oven to 200°C/400°F/gas 6.

Place the fish fillets in a casserole. Mix the tomatoes with the beans and other vegetables and add the garlic, thyme, cinnamon and seasoning. Put the mixture around the fish and pour over the reserved tomato juice. Cover the casserole and bake in the oven for 30–35 minutes.

Garnish with parsley and lemon wedges.

Accompany with Parsley rice (see page 46).

Caribbean chicken   See photograph, page 83

Serves 4–6
4 servings   Each serving: 640 kcal/2690 kJ, 34 g fibre, 11 g fat
6 servings   Each serving: 430 kcal/1800 kJ, 23 g fibre, 7 g fat

450 g/1 lb red kidney beans, soaked (see page 28)
15 ml/1 tbsp corn oil
340 g/12 oz chicken, cut in neat cubes
2 medium-sized onions, finely chopped
1 clove garlic, crushed
500 ml/18 fl oz chicken stock

2 medium-sized red peppers, chopped
60 g/2 oz lean cooked ham, chopped
4 medium-sized fresh or canned tomatoes, chopped
30 g/1 oz seedless raisins, roughly chopped
2 tbsp capers, roughly chopped
1½ tbsp oregano

¼ tsp (approx) Tabasco sauce
30 ml/2 tbsp tomato purée
seasoning
600 g/1 lb 5 oz potatoes, quartered

100 g/3½ oz fresh pineapple or canned
    pineapple without added sugar, cut
    in chunks
10 stuffed olives, sliced

Cook the beans (see page 28).

Meanwhile, heat the oil in a flameproof casserole and gently cook the chicken until lightly browned. Remove with a slotted spoon and set aside on a plate. Add the onions, garlic and 60 ml/ 4 tbsp stock to the casserole. Stir well, lower the heat and cook slowly for 15–20 minutes until the onion is tender but not brown.

Mix in the peppers, ham, tomatoes, raisins, capers, oregano, Tabasco, tomato purée, seasonings, remaining stock and the chicken. Bring to the boil, cover the casserole and simmer for 20 minutes.

Add the potatoes and cooked beans and simmer for 20–30 minutes or until the potatoes are cooked. Arrange the pineapple chunks over the top and press partly down into the mixture, then sprinkle the olives over and serve.

Baked chicken and orange

Serves 4
Each serving: 370 kcal/1550 kJ, 7 g fibre, 13 g fat

400 g/14 oz canned sweetcorn
    kernels
8 tbsp wholemeal breadcrumbs
2 tsp finely grated orange rind
1 medium-sized onion, finely chopped
2 tbsp fresh parsley and thyme, mixed
    and chopped
½ egg, beaten
seasoning

1 small roasting chicken (about
    1 kg/2.2 lb)
3 tbsp low-fat margarine spread
2 tbsp chopped parsley
juice of 2 oranges

Garnish
sprigs of watercress

Heat the oven to 190°C/375°F/gas 5.

Drain the sweetcorn and mix 3 tbsp with the breadcrumbs, orange rind, onion, herbs, egg and seasoning. Stuff the chicken with this and put in a roasting tin.

Melt the margarine, mix in the parsley and orange juice, season lightly and pour over the chicken. Roast for 1–1¼ hours, basting frequently.

Heat the remaining sweetcorn and serve around the chicken. Garnish with sprigs of watercress.

Note: For a small dinner party, suitable accompaniments would be Brown rice with orange (see page 44). The sweetcorn and the Brown rice with orange could be mixed together and interspaced with sprigs of watercress.

Veal escalopes with mushrooms and green beans

Serves 4
Each serving: 250 kcal/1050 kJ, 5 g fibre, 6 g fat

4 veal escalopes, 115 g/4 oz each, beaten flat
15 ml/1 tbsp polyunsaturated oil
1 medium-sized onion, finely chopped
45 ml/3 tbsp water
30 ml/2 tbsp dry sherry
225 g/8 oz mushrooms, sliced
300 ml/½ pint low-fat plain yoghurt
1 tbsp chopped parsley

seasoning
400 g/14 oz green beans, sliced and cooked

Marinade
30 ml/2 tbsp lemon juice
1 clove garlic, crushed
pepper

First make the marinade by mixing the ingredients together. Sprinkle the marinade over the veal, cover and leave for 1 hour. Drain.

Heat the oil in a non-stick frying pan and fry the escalopes for 3–4 minutes or until brown on both sides. Transfer to a heated serving dish and keep warm.

Put the water in the frying pan and boil, stirring, for about 1 minute to dissolve the sediment. Add the onion and cook gently until soft and the water has evaporated. Stir in the sherry, and mushrooms. Add the yoghurt, parsley and seasoning. Heat gently but do not allow to boil. Spoon over the veal.

Arrange the cooked beans around the outside of the serving dish. Serve with plainly cooked brown rice (see page 29).

Pheasant in cider with Continental lentil bake
See photograph, page 84

Serves 4
Each serving pheasant: 330 kcal/1390 kJ, 5 g fibre, 9 g fat
Each serving lentil bake: 170 kcal/710 kJ, 7 g fibre, negligible fat

1 young pheasant
1 bay leaf
1 sprig of parsley
seasoning
2 tbsp wholemeal flour
15 ml/1 tbsp polyunsaturated oil
1 medium-sized onion, sliced
3 stalks celery, chopped
2 cooking apples, cored and chopped

300 ml/½ pint dry cider
300 ml/½ pint pheasant stock

Continental lentil bake
225 g/8 oz brown Continental lentils
150 ml/¼ pint pheasant stock
1 tbsp finely chopped onion
4 tbsp chopped parsley

Joint the pheasant, removing the legs and cutting the breast section in two along the backbone. Put the carcass and cleaned giblets in a saucepan. Cover with 600 ml/1 pint water and add the bay leaf, parsley and seasoning. Simmer, partly covered for 45 minutes. Strain the stock.

Heat the oven to 170°C/325°F/gas 3.

Coat the pheasant joints with flour. Heat the oil in a non-stick casserole and fry the pheasant joints until golden brown. Lower the heat and add the onions, celery and apples. Cook, stirring occasionally, until the vegetables and apple are soft. Add the cider and stock. Cover and bake in the oven for 1 hour or until tender.

Meanwhile, cook the lentils (see page 28) and drain well. Put the the lentils in an ovenproof dish, stir in the stock, onion and parsley and bake for 15–20 minutes alongside the pheasant until the stock is absorbed. Serve hot as an accompaniment to the pheasant.

Brown rice with orange (see page 44) could also accompany the pheasant.

Strawberries in champagne

Serves 4   See photograph, page 84
Each serving: 120 kcal/500 kJ, 2 g fibre, negligible fat

30 ml/2 tbsp orange juice
*1 miniature bottle orange-flavoured
    liqueur*
*sugar or sugar-free sweetener (optional),
    to taste*

*400 g/14 oz small strawberries, or
    large strawberries, halved*
*300 ml/½ pint champagne or sparkling
    wine, chilled*

Mix the orange juice, liqueur and sugar or sweetener, if used. Sprinkle over the strawberries. Cover and leave in the refrigerator, turning occasionally. Just before serving, put into tall glasses, pour the champagne or sparkling wine over and serve.

Alternatively, serve in the shells of four orange halves.

Peach Cardinal

Serves 4
Each serving: 80 kcal/340 kJ, 6 g fibre, 2 g fat

450 g/1 lb fresh peach halves*
few drops vanilla essence
200 g/7 oz fresh or frozen raspberries

sugar or sugar-free sweetener, to taste
10 ml/2 tsp pure kirsch (optional)
2 tbsp flaked almonds, chopped

Poach the peaches in vanilla-flavoured water, chill well and place in a glass dish. Meanwhile, reserve a few raspberries for decoration

---

Caribbean chicken (see page 79)
Overleaf: Pheasant in cider with Continental lentil bake (*top left*, see page 81); Birthday cheesecake (*top right*, see page 87); Chicken and tarragon pâté (*bottom left*, see page 77); Strawberries in champagne (*bottom right*)

and purée the remainder mixed with a little of the liquid from the peaches. Stir in the sugar or sweetener and kirsch (if using). Cover the peaches with the raspberry purée – sprinkle with chopped almonds. Scatter the whole raspberries on top and serve.

*Peach halves canned without sugar may be used. Alternatively use pears, strawberries or melon balls.

Fresh fruit salad

Serves 4
Each serving: 90 kcal/380 kJ, 3 g fibre, negligible fat

2 eating apples, cored but not peeled, diced
1 orange, peeled and segmented
60 g/2 oz black grapes, halved and seeded
60 g/2 oz green grapes, halved and seeded

1 medium-sized banana
30 ml/2 tbsp orange-flavoured liqueur, maraschino or brandy (optional)
300 ml/½ pint low-calorie sparkling orange drink

Mix together the apples, oranges and grapes. Sprinkle with the liqueur or brandy, if using. Set aside for 1–2 hours to allow the flavours to develop. Just before serving, slice the banana with a fork to give a serrated effect and add to the other fruit. Pour over the sparkling orange and serve with low-calorie sorbet or cream substitute (see pages 92 and 93).

Birthday cheesecake See photograph, page 84

Serves 12
Each serving: 100 kcal/420 kJ, 5 g fibre, 3 g fat

125 g/4½ oz wholemeal breadcrumbs, toasted
2 tbsp natural bran flakes
1 tsp ground cinnamon
60 g/2 oz low-fat margarine spread
200 g/7 oz skimmed milk curd cheese
300 ml/½ pint low-fat plain yoghurt
100 ml/3½ fl oz fresh orange juice

sugar or sugar-free sweetener, to taste
3 tsp gelatine dissolved in 60 ml/4 tbsp hot water
450 g/1 lb fresh or frozen raspberries
1 egg white, whisked
225 g/8 oz large strawberries, halved
15 ml/1 tbsp brandy or pure kirsch (optional)

Mix the breadcrumbs with the bran, cinnamon and low-fat margarine. Press into the base of a 23–25 cm/9–10 inch flan tin and leave to cool. Mix the cheese, yoghurt, orange juice and sugar or sweetener together. Blend the dissolved gelatine into the cheese mixture. Mix in the raspberries, fold in the egg white and pour the mixture on to the base. Leave in the refrigerator until set.

Meanwhile, sprinkle the strawberries with the brandy or kirsch,

Orange and lemon sorbet (*top*, see page 92); Apricot whip (*centre*, see page 88); Pancakes with black cherry jam and liqueur (*bottom*, see page 89)

if using, and set aside, turning occasionally, while the cheesecake is setting. Decorate the top of the cake with these strawberries before serving.

Caribbean rumba

Serves 8
Each serving: 90 kcal/380 kJ, 2 g fibre, 2 g fat

300 g/10½ oz ripe peeled bananas
100 g/3½ oz fresh pineapple, or canned without sugar
30 ml/2 tbsp lemon juice
30 ml/2 tbsp rum
150 ml/¼ pint well-chilled evaporated milk

3 tsp gelatine dissolved in 60 ml/ 4 tbsp water
2 tbsp flaked almonds, toasted and finely chopped
60 g/4 tbsp sugar or sugar-free sweetener, to taste

Purée the banana and pineapple together in a blender and stir in the lemon juice and rum. Whisk the milk and the dissolved gelatine together and fold into the fruit purée, with the chopped almonds and sugar or sweetener. Pour into freezer trays and freeze without stirring.

Alternatively, the ice cream can be frozen in a mould and, when turned out, decorated with fruit such as red currants, dessert cherries on the stalk or strawberries.

DESSERTS

Apricot whip

See photograph, page 86

Serves 4
Each serving: 120 kcal/500 kJ, 10 g fibre, 2 g fat

150 g/5 oz dried apricots, soaked and drained
400 ml/14 fl oz water
30 ml/2 tbsp lemon juice
1 tsp ground ginger

30 g/2 tbsp sugar or sugar-free sweetener, to taste
150 ml/¼ pint low-fat plain yoghurt
2 egg whites, stiffly beaten
1 tbsp walnuts, finely chopped

Put the apricots, water and lemon juice in a saucepan and simmer for 20–30 minutes, or until tender. Purée the apricots in a blender and leave to cool.

Mix the ginger and sugar or sweetener with the yoghurt and stir into the apricot mixture. Fold in the egg whites and spoon into individual dishes and chill. Sprinkle with the walnuts before serving.

Banana yoghurt

Serves 4
Each serving: 120 kcal/500 kJ, 4 g fibre, 2 g fat

400 g/14 oz peeled bananas
300 ml/½ pint low-fat plain yoghurt
30 g/2 tbsp sugar or sugar-free

sweetener, to taste
15 ml/1 tbsp lemon juice
2 tbsp hazelnuts, finely chopped

Reserve one small banana. Slice the remainder and stir into the yoghurt along with the sugar or sweetener. Pile into serving glasses.

Slice the remaining banana, dip into the lemon juice and use to decorate. Sprinkle the hazelnuts over the top before serving.

Pancakes   See photograph, page 86

Makes 8
Each pancake: 70 kcal/290 kJ, 1 g fibre, 2 g fat

100 g/3½ oz wholemeal flour
¼ tsp salt
1 egg

1 egg white
300 ml/½ pint skimmed milk
5 ml/1 tsp polyunsaturated oil

Place the flour and salt into a bowl, make a well in the centre and drop in the egg and egg white. Gradually add one-third of the milk to the egg and beat slowly incorporating the flour, until the batter is smooth. Stir in the remaining milk and the oil, transfer to a jug, cover and set aside for 30 minutes. Stir before using.

Use a good quality non-stick frying pan measuring 15–17 cm/ 6–7 inch. Make the pancakes in the usual way, using a small ladle to transfer the batter to the pan. Stack flat until ready to serve.

Serve with slices of orange or lemon. Pancakes may also be rolled up and stuffed with a sweet or savoury filling.

Note: Pancakes may be made in advance. Stack flat on a plate, wrap in foil and store in the refrigerator. Reheat, still wrapped in foil, over a pan of boiling water.

Blackcurrant cheesecake

Serves 6
Each serving: 210 kcal/880 kJ, 7 g fibre, 8 g fat

3 tbsp low-fat margarine spread
100 g/3½ oz digestive biscuits, crushed
225 g/8 oz quark or other low-fat curd cheese
300 ml/½ pint low-fat plain yoghurt
100 ml/3½ fl oz orange juice

sugar or sugar-free sweetener, to taste
3 tsp gelatine dissolved in 60 ml/4 tbsp hot water
1 egg white, whisked
450 g/1 lb blackcurrants
1 tbsp cornflour

Melt the margarine and mix in the biscuit crumbs. Press into the base of a medium-sized flan dish and leave to cool

Mix together the cheese, yoghurt, orange juice and sugar or sweetener. Beat the dissolved gelatine into the cheese mixture. Fold in the egg white and spread over the prepared base and chill.

Stew the blackcurrants in a little water for a few minutes until they begin to soften. Add a little sugar or sweetener. Mix the cornflour to a paste with a little cold water and add to the blackcurrants. Bring to the boil and stir constantly until thickened. Cool and spread over the filling. Chill slightly before serving.

Turkish apricot and orange dessert

Serves 4–6
4 servings   Each serving: 140 kcal/590 kJ, 15 g fibre, 1 g fat
6 servings   Each serving: 100 kcal/420 kJ, 10 g fibre, 1 g fat

250 g/9 oz apricots, soaked in 500 ml/   Topping:
*   18 fl oz water*   *60 g/2 oz skimmed milk cheese (see*
grated rind and juice of 1 orange   *   page 25)*
sugar or sugar-free sweetener, to taste   *85 ml/3 fl oz low-fat plain yoghurt*
*   sugar or sugar-free sweetener, to taste*

Cook the apricots gently in the soaking liquor for 20–30 minutes or until tender. Add the orange rind and all but 30 ml/2 tbsp of the juice, allow to cool slightly and sweeten to taste. Reserve 4 or 6 apricots, purée the remainder and pour into individual glasses.

For the topping, purée the cheese, yoghurt, the reserved orange juice and sugar or sweetener in the blender. Spoon over the apricot purée, place the reserved apricots, rounded-side up, on the centre of each dish. Chill slightly before serving.

Fromage blanc and fruit

Serves 6
Each serving: 100 kcal/420 kJ, 9 g fibre, 2 g fat

6 tbsp coarse oatmeal   *680 g/1½ lb fresh or frozen raspberries*
sugar or sugar-free sweetener, to taste   *   or other soft fruit*
250 g/9 oz fromage blanc* or Cream
*   substitute II (see page 92)*

Toast the oatmeal lightly under a slow grill and set aside to cool. Add sugar or sweetener to the fromage blanc, then gently stir in the toasted oatmeal and half the raspberries. Put a spoonful of the

*Other skimmed milk curd cheese may be used.

remaining raspberries into each of the 6 tall glasses, then half the fromage blanc mixture, followed by another spoonful of raspberries. Fill up with the remaining fromage blanc mixture and decorate the top with the rest of the raspberries. Serve well chilled.

Ice creams

- Turn the freezer/refrigerator control to the coldest level.
- Made in advance, ice creams will keep their flavour for a month if stored in the deep-freeze.
- Allow 2–4 hours for the complete freezing process. Several factors cause time variations, for example, shallow metal containers (ice trays) will freeze mixtures more quickly than polythene containers; the temperature in the freezer or ice-making compartment can vary – obviously the colder the temperature, the quicker the ice cream will freeze.
- Allow ice cream to soften slightly in the refrigerator for 1–1½ hours before serving.
- Gelatine is added to sugar-free ice creams to give smoothness and to help prevent the formation of ice crystals.
- 100 g/3½ oz of fruit yields approximately 50 ml/1⅔ fl oz of purée.
- Remember to slightly over-sweeten as sweetness is reduced in freezing.

Vanilla ice cream

Serves 8
Each serving: 60 kcal/250 kJ, 0 g fibre, 3 g fat

2 tsp gelatine dissolved in 30 ml/2 tbsp hot water
300 ml/½ pint well-chilled evaporated milk
5 ml/1 tsp vanilla essence
sugar or sugar-free sweetener, to taste

Whisk the milk and almost cold gelatine together until thick and light, and add the flavouring and sugar or sweetener. Pour into freezing trays and freeze without stirring. Serve with fruit or fruit purée.

Coffee ice cream

Serves 8
Each serving: as Vanilla ice cream (above)

Make as for Vanilla ice cream, adding 1½–2 tbsp instant coffee dissolved in 45 ml/3 tbsp of the milk, then whisked into the milk mixture.

Lemon sorbet

See photograph, page 86

Serves 4

This recipe has negligible kcal/kJ, fibre and fat

finely grated rind of 1 lemon
300 ml/½ pint water
2 tsp gelatine soaked in 30 ml/2 tbsp
cold water

75 ml/5 tbsp lemon juice
sugar or sugar-free sweetener, to taste
1 egg white, lightly beaten

Bring the lemon rind and water to the boil, then allow to cool a little. Add the soaked gelatine and stir until it dissolves. Cool, and mix in the lemon juice, sugar or sweetener and egg white.

Pour into a rigid container, cover and freeze until it begins to set around the edges. Turn out into a chilled bowl and whisk until it is thick and white. Return to the container, cover and freeze until firm.

Allow to soften slightly in the refrigerator for 30–60 minutes before serving. Spoon into serving glasses or use in place of cream on cold sweets.

Orange sorbet

See photograph, page 86

Serves 4

Each serving: 10 kcal/42 kJ, negligible fibre and fat

finely grated rind of 2 oranges
240 ml/8 fl oz water
2 tsp gelatine soaked in 30 ml/
2 tbsp water

juice of 2 medium-sized oranges
sugar or sugar-free sweetener, to taste
1 egg white, lightly beaten

Make and use as for Lemon sorbet above.

Cream substitute I

Each 30 ml/2 tbsp: 20 kcal/80 kJ, 0 g fibre, 1 g fat

100 ml/3½ fl oz well-chilled
evaporated milk

sugar or sugar-free sweetener, to taste
flavouring, to taste

Whip the chilled milk until it is smooth and thick, and has trebled in volume. Add sugar or sweetener and flavouring. This can be kept in a covered container for a few days in the refrigerator.

Cream substitute II

Each 30 ml/2 tbsp: 20 kcal/80 kJ, 0 g fibre, 1 g fat

150 ml/¼ pint low-fat plain yoghurt
120 g/4¼ oz low-fat plain cottage
cheese

22 ml/1½ tbsp lemon juice or mixture
of lemon and orange juice

sugar or sugar-free sweetener, to taste
flavouring, to taste

Purée the ingredients in a blender until smooth and resembling the texture of lightly whipped cream. This can be kept in a covered container for a few days in the refrigerator.

BAKING

In yeast cookery, ensure that all utensils used are warm and the area for preparation is free from cold draughts.

Wholemeal soda bread   See photograph, page 95

Makes 2 loaves
Each 30 g/1 oz slice: 60 kcal/250 kJ, 2 g fibre, negligible fat

450 g/1 lb wholemeal flour   *1 tsp bicarbonate of soda*
1 tsp salt   *250 ml/9 fl oz buttermilk*
1 tsp cream of tartar

Heat the oven to 250°C/425°F/gas 7.
    Mix all the dry ingredients together. Add the buttermilk and mix to a light elastic dough. Divide the mixture in two and shape into rounds. Place on a floured baking tray and mark each round into four sections with a knife. Bake for 30–40 minutes until firm and well-browned. Cool on a wire rack. For a softer crust wrap in a tea towel to cool.
    This recipe can also be made using 250 ml/9 fl oz skimmed milk instead of buttermilk and 2 tsp cream of tartar.

Quick wholemeal bread

Makes 1 loaf
Each 30 g/1 oz slice: 55 kcal/230 kJ, 2 g fibre, 1 g fat

1 tsp sugar
250 ml/9 fl oz (approx) lukewarm   *450 g/1 lb wholemeal flour*
    water   *1 tsp salt*
1½ tsp dried yeast or 15 g/½ oz   *1 tbsp polyunsaturated margarine*
    fresh yeast

Dissolve the sugar in the lukewarm water, stir into the yeast and leave in a warm place for 10–15 minutes until frothy.
    In a large bowl, mix the flour with the salt and rub in the margarine. Beat the yeast liquid into the flour to form a dough. Turn on to a lightly-floured surface and knead by folding the dough towards you, then pushing away with the palm of the hand

for about 10 minutes, until firm and elastic. Place the dough in a bowl, cover with lightly-oiled polythene and leave to rise in a warm place for 1–1½ hours or until double in size.

Turn the dough on to a lightly-floured surface and knead for about 2 minutes until firm. Shape to fit a lightly-greased 450 g/1 lb non-stick loaf tin, cover with oiled polythene and leave in a warm place for about 45 minutes or until the dough is just rounded over the top of the tin.

Heat the oven to 230°C/450°F/gas 8. Bake the loaf for 30–40 minutes until it is golden brown and sounds hollow if tapped underneath. Cool on a wire rack.

Variations

Rolls: Divide the 450 g/1 lb wholemeal bread recipe dough into 12 and shape into small rolls. Place on a floured baking tray 1.5 cm/¾ inch apart for soft-sided rolls or 2.5 cm/1 inch apart for crusty rolls. Cover with lightly-oiled polythene and leave in a warm place until doubled in size. Bake at 230°C/450°F/gas 8 for 20–25 minutes.

French onion bread: Use the 450 g/1 lb quantity wholemeal yeast bread recipe. Add 3 tbsp finely chopped onion plus 1 crushed garlic clove sautéed in 15 ml/1 tbsp corn oil, to the yeast, sugar and water mixture when it has become frothy.

Instead of baking the loaf in a tin, shape into an oval or baton shape and place on a non-stick baking sheet. Make small diagonal cuts on top before covering and leaving to rise. Brush the surface with equal quantities of beaten egg white and water. Bake on the middle shelf of the oven at 190°C/375°F/gas 5 for 25–30 minutes. Cool on a wire rack.

Breadsticks: These can be made by reserving part of the mixed yeast dough at the stage where the dough has risen to double its size.

Knead the dough on a floured board and roll out to 20 × 22.5 cm/8 × 9 inch. Cut into strips about 1 cm/½ inch wide and roll each into a stick. Place on a lightly-greased tray and bake in a hot oven until crisp.

Norwegian bread

Makes 1 loaf
Each 30 g/1 oz slice: 65 kcal/270 kJ, 2 g fibre, 1 g fat

1 tsp sugar	*25 g/¾ oz dried yeast*
150 ml/¼ pint (approx) lukewarm	*450 g/1 lb wholemeal flour*
water	*3 tbsp rye flour*

Wholemeal soda bread (*top left*, see page 93); Norwegian bread (*top right*); Date and rhubarb cake (*bottom*, see page 99)

3 tbsp wheat germ
3 tbsp natural bran flakes
1 tsp salt

1 tbsp polyunsaturated margarine
150 ml/¼ pint skimmed milk

Dissolve the sugar in the water, stir into the yeast and leave in a warm place for 10 minutes or until frothy. In a large bowl, mix together the flours, wheat germ, bran flakes and salt and rub in the margarine. Add the milk to the yeast mixture and beat into the flour, adding extra water if necessary to form a soft dough. Knead well. Cover with polythene and leave in a warm place for 45–60 minutes or until the dough has risen to double its size.

Turn out the dough on to a lightly-floured surface and knead for about 5 minutes. Shape to fit a non-stick 450 g/1 lb loaf tin. Cover and leave again in a warm place for 30–45 minutes or until the dough is just rounded over the top of the tin.

Heat the oven to 220°C/425°F/gas 7. Bake the loaf for 30–40 minutes until it is golden brown and sounds hollow if tapped underneath. Cool on a wire rack.

Wholemeal buttermilk scones

Makes 12
Each scone: 80 kcal/340 kJ, 3 g fibre, 3 g fat

200 g/7 oz wholemeal flour
4 tbsp natural bran flakes
1 tsp bicarbonate of soda
1 tsp cream of tartar
½ tsp salt
30 g/1 oz polyunsaturated margarine

sugar or sugar-free sweetener, to taste
(optional)
150 ml/¼ pint buttermilk or soured
skimmed milk, or use fresh skimmed
milk and 1 extra tsp cream of
tartar

Heat the oven to 220°C/425°F/gas 7.

Mix the dry ingredients together in a bowl and rub in the margarine until the mixture resembles fine breadcrumbs. Add the sugar or sweetener, if using, to the milk and stir into the flour to form a soft dough. Roll out lightly on a floured board to 12 mm/ ½ inch thick and cut into rounds using a 5 cm/2 inch cutter. Place on a non-stick baking tray, brush with a little milk and bake for 8– 10 minutes. Cool on a wire rack.

Fruit scones Add 30 g/1 oz raisins or sultanas, chopped, to the rubbed-in mixture.

Date scones Add 45 g/1½ oz dates, chopped, to the rubbed-in mixture.

Oxford muesli (*top*, see page 110); Toasted turkey sandwich (*centre*, see page 108); Quick pizza (*bottom*, see page 109)

Oat popovers

Makes 12
Each popover: 70 kcal/290 kJ, 4 g fibre, 2 g fat

45 g/1½ oz rolled oats
70 g/2½ oz wholemeal flour
2 tsp baking powder
85 g/3 oz natural bran flakes
1 tsp mixed spice (optional)
2 tsp grated orange rind (optional)

45 g/1½ oz sugar or sugar-free
*   sweetener, to taste*
1 egg, beaten
300 ml/½ pint skimmed milk
10 ml/2 tsp polyunsaturated oil

Heat the oven to 200°C/400°F/gas 6.
   Place the dry ingredients in a bowl. Add the sugar or sweetener to the egg, milk and oil and beat together. Mix into the dry ingredients. Divide the mixture between 12 non-stick patty tins and bake for 25–30 minutes. Serve hot, cold or toasted for breakfast, or for a small snack at any time of day.

Note: To make **date popovers**, add 70 g/2½ oz chopped dates to the dry ingredients and continue as Oat popovers above.
Each popover: 90 kcal/380 kJ, 5 g fibre, 2 g fat

Wholesome fingers

Makes 24
Each finger: 90 kcal/380 kJ, 2 g fibre, 4 g fat

200 g/7 oz wholemeal flour
2 tsp baking powder
pinch salt
100 g/3½ oz polyunsaturated
*   margarine*
sugar or sugar-free sweetener, to taste
70 g/2½ oz mashed potato (or instant,
*   reconstituted)*

200 g/7 oz carrots, grated
100 g/3½ oz chestnuts, cooked, skinned
*   and finely chopped**
70 g/2½ oz stoneless dates, chopped
70 g/2½ oz sultanas, chopped
¼ tsp ground cinnamon
¼ tsp ground mace
2 eggs, beaten

Heat the oven to 180°C/350°F/gas 4.
   Mix the flour, baking powder and salt in a bowl and rub in the margarine until the mixture resembles fine breadcrumbs. Beat the sugar or sweetener into the potatoes and mix into the flour, together with the carrots, chestnuts, dates, sultanas and spices. Beat in the eggs to form a fairly stiff consistency. Spread in a non-stick 18 × 20 cm/7 × 11 inch tin and bake for 30–35 minutes. Leave to cool in the tin, then cut into 24 fingers.

*Canned sugar-free chestnuts or dried reconstituted chestnuts can be used instead.

Nutty oatmeal biscuits

Makes 30
Each biscuit: 50 kcal/210 kJ, 9 g fibre, 2 g fat

*100 g/3½ oz wholemeal self-raising
  flour
½ tsp baking powder
½ tsp powdered cinnamon
60 g/2 oz hazelnuts, chopped
60 g/2 oz seedless raisins, chopped
60 ml/4 tbsp skimmed milk
60 ml/4 tbsp apple juice*

*150 g/5 oz rolled oats
1 egg white, lightly beaten
1–2 tsp orange rind
5–10 ml/1–2 tsp rum or other
  flavouring
30 ml/2 tbsp polyunsaturated oil
1 eating apple, cored and finely
  chopped*

Heat the oven to 190°C/375°F/gas 5.
  Mix together the flour, baking powder, cinnamon, nuts and raisins in a bowl. In a separate bowl, stir the milk and apple juice into the rolled oats and mix well together. Stir in the egg white, orange rind, rum or other flavouring and oil. Beat in the flour mixture. Stir in the chopped apple. The mixture will have a thick consistency.
  Place spoonfuls on an ungreased baking tray, leaving room for the biscuits to spread. Bake for approximately 20 minutes. Cool the biscuits on a rack and, when cold, store in an airtight container.

Date and rhubarb cake See photograph, page 95

Makes 12 slices
Each slice: 140 kcal/590 kJ, 4 g fibre, 5 g fat

*225 g/8 oz rhubarb, chopped
225 g/8 oz wholemeal flour
3 tsp baking powder
60 g/2 oz polyunsaturated margarine*

*170 g/6 oz stoneless dates, chopped
1 egg, beaten
60 ml/4 tbsp skimmed milk*

Heat the oven to 190°C/375°F/gas 5.
  Cook the rhubarb in a little water for 5–10 minutes and drain. Put the flour and baking powder in a bowl and rub in the margarine until the mixture resembles fine breadcrumbs. Stir in the dates and rhubarb. Add the egg and milk and mix well. Put into a 20 cm sq/8 inch sq non-stick cake tin and bake for 1 hour. Divide into 12 slices when cool.

Sweet or savoury flan case

Serves 4–6
4 servings   Each serving: 150 kcal/630 kJ, 3 g fibre, 6 g fat
6 servings   Each serving: 100 kcal/420 kJ, 2 g fibre, 4 g fat

115 g/4 oz wholemeal flour   *2 tbsp polyunsaturated margarine*
1 tsp baking powder   *cold water to mix*
pinch salt

Heat the oven to 200°C/400°F/gas 6.

Mix the flour, baking powder and salt together in a bowl. Rub in the margarine until the mixture resembles fine breadcrumbs. Add a little water and knead to a stiff dough. Roll to the required size between sheets of greaseproof paper. Peel off the top sheet of paper, lift the dough, still on the bottom layer of paper and invert to line an 18–20 cm/7–8 inch flan dish. Remove the paper. Prick the base and bake blind for 20–25 minutes.

For a savoury flan case, flavoured salt can be substituted for ordinary salt and ¼ tsp dried mustard or about 1 tbsp finely chopped fresh herbs added.

DRESSINGS AND SAUCES

DRESSINGS

Lowest in fat and simple to make are seasoned yoghurt dressings. To make, stir all the ingredients into the yoghurt and mix well. Used in small quantities, they do not have to be included in slimmers' daily calculations.

Basic yoghurt dressing

150 ml/¼ pint low-fat plain yoghurt   *¼ tsp salt*
15 ml/1 tbsp lemon juice   *pepper*
½ tsp prepared mustard

Additions
Add one or more of the following: finely chopped onions, cucumber or peppers; ½–1 clove garlic, crushed; garlic, onion or celery salt in place of plain salt; 2–3 drops Tabasco sauce; 15 ml/1 tbsp tomato ketchup (sugar-free) or chilli sauce; sugar-free proprietary salad seasonings and mixes.

Curry dressing

150 ml/¼ pint low-fat plain yoghurt   *1 tbsp chopped unsweetened pickle*
15 ml/1 tbsp lemon juice   *¼ tsp salt*

pepper
2–3 drops sugar-free sweetener

2 tsp curry powder
other curry spices, if liked

Piquant dressing

150 ml/¼ pint low-fat plain yoghurt
½ tsp prepared mustard
¼ tsp garlic salt

2 tsp Worcester sauce
2–3 drops Tabasco sauce

Green dressing

150 ml/¼ pint low-fat plain yoghurt
¼ tsp garlic salt
½ tsp prepared mustard
2 tbsp finely chopped onion
2 tbsp chopped gherkins
2 tbsp chopped capers or other sugar-free green pickles

4 tbsp chopped parsley or mixture of parsley and other green herbs, the type depending on the dish it is to accompany
15 ml/1 tbsp lemon juice, or vinegar from jar of pickles

Add all the ingredients to the yoghurt and mix. Alternatively, put all the ingredients (unchopped) into a blender and purée to a smooth consistency. Use as a dressing or sauce with fish, chicken and cold meats.

French dressing

60 ml/4 tbsp wine or tarragon vinegar or lemon juice or a mixture of these
½ tsp salt or garlic or celery salt
¼ tsp pepper

½ tsp prepared mustard
60 ml/4 tbsp sunflower or other polyunsaturated oil
2 tbsp chopped herbs (optional)

Put all ingredients into a screw-top jar and shake well. Store in the refrigerator.

SAUCES

Tomato sauce

Serves 4
Each serving: 50 kcal/210 kJ, 1 g fibre, 4 g fat

15 ml/1 tbsp polyunsaturated oil
1 medium-sized onion, finely chopped
75 ml/5 tbsp tomato purée

pinch of thyme
300 ml/½ pint water
seasoning

Heat the oil in a saucepan. Add the onion and fry gently for 5 minutes until transparent. Add the tomato purée and cook for a few minutes, stirring. Stir in the thyme and water, cover and simmer gently for 25–30 minutes. Season to taste before serving.

Barbecue sauce

Serves 6
Each serving: 10 kcal/40 kJ, 1 g fibre, 0 g fat

225 g/8 oz canned tomatoes, chopped   ½ tsp dried basil
*   with juice   1 clove garlic, crushed*
2 medium-sized onions, chopped   seasoning

Put all the ingredients into a saucepan and simmer together until thick and pulpy. Purée in a blender and adjust the seasoning before serving.

White sauce

Serves 4
Each serving: 50 kcal/210 kJ, negligible fibre, 2 g fat

250 ml/9 fl oz skimmed milk   1½ tbsp wholemeal flour
10 ml/2 tsp polyunsaturated oil or   seasoning
*   margarine*

Put the milk and oil or margarine into a saucepan and gradually whisk in the flour. Heat gently, whisking constantly until the mixture thickens and boils. Cook for 3 minutes, then season.

Variations

Anchovy sauce: Add 5–10 ml/1–2 tsp anchovy essence.

Caper sauce: Add 2 tbsp roughly-chopped capers and, if liked, 5 ml/1 tsp caper vinegar.

Parsley sauce: Add 2–3 tbsp freshly-chopped parsley and, if liked, 5 ml/1 tsp lemon juice.

Onion sauce: Add 150 g/5 oz onion, boiled, drained and chopped and ¼ tsp onion or garlic salt.

Fruit sauce for ice cream
Total recipe: 60 kcal/250 kJ, 15 g fibre, 0 g fat

*200 g/7 oz ripe blackberries**
sugar or sugar-free sweetener, to taste

Wash fruit, remove stalks and place in an electric blender. Purée to a pulp, sweeten and serve.

Note: Other fruits (fresh, canned in natural juice or stewed) may be used instead. For example: cherries, black or red currants, raspberries, strawberries and so on. Try unusual mixtures such as puréed dried (and cooked) fruit salad or a delicate-flavoured fruit such as stewed pears.

*½–1 tbsp of kirsch or other liqueur may be added.

SNACKS

Low-calorie liver pâté

Each 30 g/1 oz: 40 kcal/170 kJ, negligible fibre, 2 g fat

200 g/7 oz ox liver
1 stalk celery
2 tbsp chopped parsley
1 tbsp chopped onion

*150 ml/5 oz condensed tomato soup**
(different flavours of condensed soup
can be used)

Remove veins and skin from the liver and mince finely, then put the celery, parsley and onion through the mincer. Stir into the soup and cook, beating well, for 10 minutes. Adjust seasoning and press into a bowl or small pots. Cool, cover and keep in the refrigerator.

*To make a softer pâté, add 30 ml/2 tbsp extra soup and use as a spread.

Red bean pâté

Each 30 g/1 oz: 50 kcal/210 kJ, 1 g fibre, 2 g fat

100 g/3½ oz wholemeal breadcrumbs
a little stock
a few drops soy sauce
15 ml/1 tbsp polyunsaturated oil
1 medium-sized onion, chopped

100 g/3½ oz cooked kidney beans (see
page 28), mashed
60 g/2 oz Edam-type cheese, grated
mixed herbs
seasoning

Put the breadcrumbs in a small bowl. Add a little stock and a few drops of soy sauce.

Heat the oil in a small frying pan and lightly fry the onion. Tip the onion into a bowl and combine with the beans and cheese, mixing very well. Squeeze most of the moisture from the breadcrumbs and stir into the bean mixture with herbs and seasoning to taste. Spoon into a serving dish or small pots. Store in the refrigerator until ready to serve.

Smoked mackerel pâté

Each 30 g/1 oz: 40 kcal/170 kJ, negligible fibre, 1 g fat

200 g/7 oz smoked mackerel, skinned, boned and flaked
100 g/3½ oz skimmed-milk cheese, sieved if necessary (see page 25)
15 ml/1 tbsp low-calorie proprietary vinaigrette
15 ml/1 tbsp lemon juice
5 ml/1 tsp anchovy essence
seasoning and pinch of nutmeg

Put the mackerel and cheese in a bowl and mash together well. Then thoroughly mix in the remaining ingredients, or mix all ingredients together in a blender. Adjust seasoning and season more highly if liked. Put into small pots or a mould and store in the refrigerator.

Canned, drained tuna fish, pilchards or salmon may be used instead of the mackerel. For special occasions, strips of anchovy fillets may be used to garnish.

Mushroom and lentil pâté

Each 30 g/1 oz: 20 kcal/80 kJ, 1 g fibre, 1 g fat

1 small onion, finely chopped
5 ml/1 tsp polyunsaturated oil
200 g/7 oz flat mushrooms
100 g/3 oz cooked brown lentils, (see page 28)
60 g/2 oz skimmed milk curd cheese
2 tbsp chopped parsley
15 ml/1 tbsp lemon juice
garlic salt
pepper
45 ml/3 tbsp canned consommé (optional)

Cook the onion in the oil in a non-stick pan until soft. Grill the mushrooms for 2 minutes under a medium grill. Put the onion, mushrooms and all the remaining ingredients in a blender and purée. Spoon into a serving dish or small pots, cover and store in the refrigerator until firm. Serve as a pâté accompanied by lettuce, tomato and cucumber, or use as a sandwich spread, toast topper or for canapés. May be garnished with mushrooms, watercress and tomato.

Low-calorie spread

2 tsp: 5 kcal/20 kJ, negligible fibre and fat

200 g/7 oz peeled, cored and sliced
sweet eating apples*
1 tsp powdered gelatine dissolved in
60 ml/4 tbsp hot water

60 g/2 oz quark or other skimmed
milk curd cheese
colouring (optional)

Put the apples and a little water in a saucepan and cook to a soft pulp. Set aside and allow to cool. Place the apple pulp in a blender with the dissolved gelatine, cheese and colouring, if used, and blend to a smooth purée. Leave to set.

Use on plain biscuits, scones and popovers or as an icing on large and small cakes. It can also be piped.

This spread, stored in a covered container, keeps well in the refrigerator and may be deep-frozen.

*Choose a variety such as Golden Delicious, which stays white when cooked; when using to spread on scones, etc, try using strawberries, damsons, etc. instead of apple.

Macaroni in curd cheese sauce

Serves 4
Each serving: 300 kcal/1260 kJ, 7 g fibre, 8 g fat

200 g/7 oz short-cut wholemeal
macaroni
1 tbsp polyunsaturated margarine
200 g/7 oz skimmed milk curd cheese
60 ml/4 tbsp skimmed milk
4 tbsp chopped red pepper
1 clove garlic, crushed

pinch dried mixed herbs
4 tbsp chopped chives
1 tbsp grated Parmesan or other low-
fat strong cheese
garlic salt
pepper

Cook the macaroni in boiling, salted water (see page 30) and drain.

Melt the margarine in a saucepan. Add the macaroni, shaking well to distribute the fat. Blend the curd cheese and milk together, stir in the pepper, garlic, herbs, chives, Parmesan cheese and seasoning. Add to the macaroni and stir gently for about 5 minutes or until heated through.

Spaghetti with meat balls and tomato sauce

Serves 4
Each serving: 340 kcal/1430 kJ, 11 g fibre, 9 g fat

200 g/7 oz cooked butter beans (see
page 28)

200 g/7 oz lean beef, finely minced
3 tbsp wholemeal breadcrumbs ◆

4 tbsp natural bran flakes
onion salt
pepper
good pinch ground mace (optional)

1 egg, beaten
450 ml/¾ pint Tomato sauce (see page 101)
500 g/18 oz wholemeal spaghetti

Mash the beans with a fork and mix in the meat, breadcrumbs, bran, seasoning, mace, if using, and the egg. Shape into 20 very small meat balls. Arrange in the grill pan and cook under a medium-hot grill, turning until well browned all over. Meanwhile, lower the spaghetti gently into a large pan of boiling salted water, and cook for 10–15 minutes or according to directions on packet. Drain and serve with meatballs and tomato sauce.

Variations

The meat balls can be served hot or cold, with or without the sauce and with or without the spaghetti.

Flavourings such as chopped vegetables, herbs and spices can be added to the meat according to taste.

Other types of lean meats (for example, liver) can be incorporated.

Chopped tomatoes, red peppers (or other vegetables) can be added to the sauce. Different varieties of wholemeal pasta can be substituted for the spaghetti.

Spaghetti with chicken and mushroom sauce

Serves 4

Each serving: 270 kcal/1130 kJ, 9 g fibre, 8 g fat

200 g/7 oz cooked chicken meat, chopped
115 g/4 oz canned mushrooms, sliced
2 tbsp dried onions
10 ml/2 tsp Worcester sauce
300 ml/½ pint White sauce (see page 102)

2 tbsp chopped parsley
½ tsp garlic salt
pepper
250 g/9 oz wholemeal spaghetti
paprika

Add the chicken, mushrooms, onions and Worcester sauce to the white sauce and simmer for about 15 minutes. Stir in the parsley, salt and pepper.

Meanwhile, cook the spaghetti in boiling salted water (see page 30). Drain and put the cooked spaghetti in a heated serving dish. Pour the chicken mixture over the spaghetti and stir to distribute evenly. Sprinkle lightly with paprika and serve.

Wholemeal spaghetti in meat sauce

Serves 4
Each serving: 400 kcal/1680 kJ, 11 g fibre, 8 g fat

15 ml/1 tbsp corn oil
170 g/6 oz lean beef, minced
2 medium-sized onions, chopped
1 clove garlic, crushed
2 medium-sized carrots, chopped
2 stalks celery, chopped

30 ml/2 tbsp tomato purée
375 ml/13 fl oz stock
1 tbsp chopped basil
2 tbsp chopped peppers
seasoning
340 g/12 oz wholemeal spaghetti

Heat the oil in a saucepan and gently cook the meat, onions, garlic, carrots and celery for 10 minutes. Stir in the tomato purée, stock, basil, peppers and seasoning and simmer for 30–40 minutes.

Meanwhile, lower the spaghetti gently into a large pan of boiling salted water and cook for 10–15 minutes or according to directions on the packet. Drain and serve with the sauce.

Wholemeal spaghetti with tomato sauce

Serves 4
Each serving: 340 kcal/1430 kJ, 10 g fibre, 6 g fat

15 ml/1 tbsp polyunsaturated oil
1 large onion, chopped
400 g/14 oz canned tomatoes, chopped
  with juice

½–1 tbsp chopped marjoram
1 tsp garlic salt
pepper
340 g/12 oz wholemeal spaghetti

Heat the oil in a saucepan and gently fry the onion until pale brown. Stir in the tomatoes and simmer for 15–20 minutes until thickened. Add the marjoram and seasoning.

Meanwhile, boil the spaghetti in salted water for 10–15 minutes or according to directions on the packet. Drain well, and serve with the sauce poured over.

Beans in tomato sauce

Serves 4
Each serving: 300 kcal/1260 kJ, 9 g fibre, 10 g fat

500 ml/18 fl oz tomato juice
1 shallot or small onion, grated or very
  finely chopped
75 ml/5 tbsp cider vinegar
10 ml/2 tsp Worcester sauce
dash Tabasco sauce
¼ tsp celery salt

seasoning
pinch dried tarragon
450 g/1 lb cooked soya beans (see
  page 28)
200 g/7 oz sliced wholemeal bread,
  toasted (see page 93)

Put the tomato juice, shallot or onion, vinegar, sauces and seasonings in a saucepan and simmer for 5 minutes. Remove from the heat, cool, then purée in a blender. Return to the pan, add the beans and cook for 10 minutes. Divide evenly between the slices of toast and serve.

Spiced soya toast topper

Serves 4
Each serving: 310 kcal/1300 kJ, 13 g fibre, 8 g fat

450 g/1 lb cooked soya beans (see page 28)
500 ml/18 fl oz tomato juice
3 tbsp dried onion flakes
1 clove garlic, crushed
2 medium-sized carrots, thinly sliced
1 tsp ground cumin
½ tsp turmeric
½ tsp ground ginger
2 tbsp chopped parsley
seasoning
1 medium-sized green pepper, chopped
4 large medium–thick slices wholemeal bread, toasted

Put all the ingredients, except the green pepper and bread, into a large bowl and mix well. Cover and set aside for 1 hour.

Transfer the mixture to a saucepan and cook gently for 30 minutes. Five minutes before serving, stir in the peppers. Spoon the mixture over the 4 toast slices and serve.

Toasted turkey sandwiches

Serves 4   See photograph, page 96
Each serving: 360 kcal/1510 kJ, 13 g fibre, 5 g fat

200 g/7 oz cooked turkey* meat, diced
45 ml/3 tbsp Basic yoghurt dressing (see page 100)
1 stalk celery, finely chopped
100 g/3½ oz quark or other low-fat curd cheese
200 g/7 oz canned sweetcorn kernels, drained
8 large slices medium-cut wholemeal bread

Garnish
4 medium-sized tomatoes, sliced
1 punnet mustard and cress

Mix together the turkey, salad dressing, celery, cheese and sweetcorn. Use to make 4 sandwiches with the wholemeal bread. Place under the grill and toast, then turn over and toast the other side. Garnish with overlapping slices of tomatoes and sprigs of cress.

Serve hot.

*Chicken or canned fish may be substituted for the turkey.

Chicken à la king

Serves 4
Each serving: 320 kcal/1340 kJ, 7 g fibre, 9 g fat

15 ml/1 tbsp polyunsaturated oil
1 onion, finely chopped
2 tbsp wholemeal flour
450 ml/¾ pint skimmed milk
200 g/7 oz cooked chicken, diced
60 g/2 oz cooked haricot or other beans, roughly chopped

100 g/3½ oz canned mushrooms, sliced
2 tbsp chopped mixed peppers
15 ml/1 tbsp dry sherry
seasoning
4 large, medium-cut slices of wholemeal bread, toasted

Heat the oil in a saucepan, add the onion, cover and cook gently until the onion is softened but not brown. Stir in the flour and cook for 1–2 minutes, then gradually stir in the milk. Bring to the boil, stirring. Lower the heat and simmer until thickened. Add the chicken, beans, mushrooms, peppers, sherry and seasoning and cook gently for 10 minutes or until all the ingredients are piping hot.

Pour over hot toast and serve accompanied by watercress or a mixed salad (see pages 36–40).

Pizza baps

Makes 8 mini pizzas
Each pizza: 130 kcal/550 kJ, 3 g fibre, 4 g fat

100 g/3½ oz fromage blanc or other low-fat curd cheese
100 g/3½ oz canned mackerel
60 g/2 oz cooked haricot or other beans
2 tbsp chopped parsley
2 tbsp chopped chives
10 ml/2 tsp lemon juice or vinegar

pepper
4 pizza baps, halved
2 medium-sized tomatoes, sliced
6 tbsp grated low-fat hard cheese
60 g/2 oz lean ham, sliced in thin strips
8 black olives, stoned and sliced (optional)

Mash together the curd cheese, mackerel, beans, herbs, lemon juice or vinegar and pepper. Spread over the halved baps, put a slice of tomato on top of each and sprinkle with grated cheese. Arrange a lattice of ham on top, garnish with the olives, if using, and cook under a grill until the cheese is golden brown.

Quick pizza
See photograph, page 96

Serves 4
Each serving: 210 kcal/880 kJ, 6 g fibre, 6 g fat

100 g/3½ oz cooked wholemeal pizza base (bought or home-made using
bread recipe page 93)

♦

Topping
1 tbsp low-fat margarine spread
1 medium-sized onion, finely chopped
150 g/5 oz canned tomatoes, drained
and chopped
1 tsp dried marjoram or dried mixed
herbs
200 g/7 oz canned red kidney or
canned mixed beans, drained

100 g/3½ oz tuna in brine, drained
and flaked
60 g/2 oz low-fat hard cheese, grated
30 g/1 oz anchovy fillets, drained and
cut in thin strips
4 stuffed olives, halved

Make the topping: Melt the margarine in a saucepan and cook
the onion until soft. Stir in the tomatoes, herbs, beans and tuna
and heat through. Spread evenly over the pizza base and sprinkle
over the cheese. Decorate with a lattice of anchovies and olives.
Place for a few minutes under a hot grill to melt the cheese. Serve
with a green salad.

Havana rice and black beans

Serves 4
Each serving: 330 kcal/1390 kJ, 13 g fibre, 5 g fat

115 g/4 oz long-grain brown rice
15 ml/1 tbsp polyunsaturated oil
1 small onion, chopped
1 small green pepper, chopped
1 clove garlic, crushed

60 ml/4 tbsp dry red wine
seasoning
1 small bay leaf
600 g/1 lb 5 oz cooked black beans, hot
(see page 28)

While the rice is cooking (see page 29), heat the oil in a saucepan.
Add the onion, pepper and garlic and fry gently until the onion is
golden brown. Add the wine, seasoning and bay leaf and continue
to cook gently for a further 10 minutes. Stir in the hot beans,
cover and cook over a moderate heat for a further 20 minutes.
Spoon the beans into the centre of a hot serving dish and surround
with the newly cooked rice. This dish may be garnished with
peppers and parsley.

Oxford muesli   See photograph, page 96

**Each 60 g/2 oz (6 tbsp) serving: 170 kcal/710 kJ, 13 g fibre, 4 g
fat**

60 g/2 oz rolled oats
60 g/2 oz cracked wheat
60 g/2 oz barley flakes
60 g/2 oz rye flakes
60 g/2 oz large natural bran flakes
60 g/2 oz soya bran

60 g/2 oz dried apricots, chopped
60 g/2 oz mixed raisins, currants and
sultanas, chopped
60 g/2 oz hazelnuts, ground or finely
chopped
¼ tsp mixed spice

Mix all the ingredients together and store in an airtight container. Serve with skimmed milk, low-fat yoghurt, yoghurt juice (sugar-free) or fresh fruit sweetened with sugar or a sugar-free sweetener if liked.

Orange yoghurt juice

Serves 8
Each serving: 60 kcal/250 kJ, negligible fibre, 1 g fat

450 ml/1 pint low-fat plain yoghurt   *sugar or sugar-free sweetener, to taste*
500 ml/18 fl oz unsweetened canned   *orange slices*
  orange juice*

Mix all the ingredients together and chill well. Serve in goblets or short glasses decorated with orange slices on the rim.

Alternatively, use in place of skimmed milk with breakfast cereals.

*Other flavours of fruit juice may be used.

DAILY MEAL PLANS

Choose 2 or 3 items for each meal

Breakfast　　Fresh or stewed fruit
Porridge or wholegrain breakfast cereal –
　Weetabix, Shredded wheat, Shreddies, Wheat
　flakes, Puffed wheat
Wheatgerm to sprinkle over cereal
Serving of protein food such as lean bacon, ham,
　fish, egg (*optional*)
Wholemeal bread, rolls, Popovers (see page 98)
　or crispbreads
Marmalade, honey or jam
Coffee, tea or fruit juice

Midmorning　Coffee or tea
Biscuit or alternative from Baking section (see
　pages 93–100, *optional*)

Midday　　　(*A snack-type meal. Alternatively, this may be eaten in the
　evening*)
Main course vegetable soup(see page 32)
Wholemeal bread, rolls or crispbread (see page
　93)
Sandwiches (see page 119) or snack recipe (see
　pages 103–111)
Wholegrain rice or pasta dish; pizza (see pages
　44–50 and 109)
Cold poultry, meat, fish; home-made pâté (see
　pages 103–4)
Vegetable dishes (see pages 41–3)
Summer or winter salad (see pages 36–40)
Fruit or fruity pudding (see pages 88–93)
Biscuit or alternative from Baking section (see
　pages 93–100)
Hot or cold drink

Afternoon　　Coffee or tea
Biscuit or alternative from Baking section (see
　pages 93–100, *optional*)

Evening　　　(*A main meal. Alternatively, this may be eaten midday*)
Vegetable soup (see page 31), fruit or fruit
　juice

Fish, poultry or meat or a dish containing any of
them
Beans, peas, sweetcorn, root vegetables, green
vegetables or a salad
Vegetable dishes (see pages 41–43)
Potatoes baked or boiled in skins; or brown rice or
pasta
Fruity pudding (see pages 88–93) or fresh fruit
Hot or cold drink

Bedtime Hot drink
Biscuit or alternative from Baking section (see
pages 93–100, *optional*)

Between Items from the Bakery section (see pages 93–100)
meal snacks Wholemeal proprietary biscuits
Wholemeal soda bread with honey (see page 93)
Dry roasted nuts (small packet), or small bowl
permitted nuts & raisins
Slimmers' crispbread, spread sparingly with low-
calorie margarine spread or slimmers proprietary salad cream or soft strong-flavoured
cheese

Daily Skimmed milk for drinks, cereals and cooking
Moderate amounts of polyunsaturated margarine
or low-fat margarine spread
Moderate amounts of polyunsaturated oil

A day's meals using recipes in this book

Breakfast   ½ grapefruit
Toasted oatmeal popovers (see page 98) with
    polyunsaturated margarine and marmalade
Coffee or tea

Midmorning   Coffee or tea

Midday   Italian vegetable soup (see page 32)
Crusty, wholemeal bread (see page 93), spread
    sparingly with Brie
Coffee or tea

Afternoon   Coffee or tea

Evening   Spanish baked fish (see page 64)
Broccoli spears
Jacket potatoes served with Basic yoghurt dress-
    ing (see page 100)
Apricot whip (see page 88)

Bedtime   Milky drink
Nutty oatmeal biscuit (see page 99)

Between   See page 113
meal snacks

Daily   Skimmed milk for cooking and drinks
Polyunsaturated margarine and low-fat margarine
    spread
Polyunsaturated oil

A day's meals using recipes in this book

Breakfast Fresh or stewed fruit
Weetabix or other wholegrain cereal (see page 112)
Crispbreads with polyunsaturated margarine and marmalade
Coffee or tea

Midmorning Coffee or tea

Midday Toasted turkey sandwich (see page 108)
or Smoked brisling, herring or mackerel with side salad (see pages 36–40)
or Smoked brisling on wholemeal toast
Fresh fruit
Hot or cold drink

Afternoon Coffee or tea

Evening **Entertaining: small dinner party**
Melon slice or melon balls
Pheasant in cider (see page 81)
Mangetout or garden peas
Baked aubergine halves garnished with chopped fresh tomatoes
New potatoes tossed in chopped parsley
Pancakes spread with black cherry jam mixed with a little liqueur, if liked (see page 89)

Bedtime Hot drink

Between meal snacks See page 113

Daily Skimmed milk for drinks, cereals and cooking
Polyunsaturated margarine or low-fat margarine spread
Polyunsaturated oil

A day's meals for a child* using the recipes in this book

Breakfast   Oxford muesli (see page 110) with milk or orange
yoghurt juice (see page 111) or proprietary low-
fat yoghurt juice
Crispy grilled bacon with grilled tomato (optional)
Wholemeal bread with polyunsaturated margarine
and preserves
Weak milky tea

Midmorning   Milk drink

Midday   Chicken casserole (see page 68)
Lightly cooked green beans
Potatoes boiled with skin and tossed in chopped
herbs
Home-made vanilla ice cream (see page 91) with
fruit sauce (see page 103)

High tea/   (This may be exchanged for the midday meal)
Supper   Spaghetti with meat balls and tomato sauce (see
page 105)
Wholemeal bread with polyunsaturated margarine
and yeast extract
or (especially if exchanged for a midday meal):
Sandwiches – wholemeal bread spread liberally
with low-fat quark and filled with chopped dates
and oranges or pineapple crush
Fresh fruit

Bedtime   Milky drink
Wholesome finger (see page 98)

Between meal snacks
This depends on the individual child – children of
the same age vary enormously in the amounts of
food they require and their need to include or
avoid between meal snacks

Daily   Include 600 ml/1 pint skimmed milk for cooking
and drinks
Polyunsaturated margarine or low-fat margarine
spread
Polyunsaturated oil

*From 5 years onwards

A day's meals for a vegetarian, using recipes in this book

Breakfast	Shreddies with 1 tbsp wheatgerm sprinkled over
	Hot wholemeal scones with polyunsaturated margarine and honey
	Coffee or tea
Mid-morning	Coffee or tea
Midday	Chick pea and leek quiche (see page 57)
	Cabbage and raisin salad (see page 38)
	Baked potato
	Banana yoghurt (see page 89)
Afternoon	Coffee or tea
Evening	Macaroni and curd cheese sauce (see page 105)
	Tomatoes Provençal (see page 42)
	Norwegian bread (see page 94)
	Fresh fruit
Bedtime	Milky drink
Between meal snacks	See page 113
Daily	Skimmed milk for drinks, cereals and cooking
	Polyunsaturated margarine or low-fat margarine spread
	Polyunsaturated oil

EATING OUT

If possible choose somewhere to eat where you know the menu will include simply-cooked food rather than elaborate made-up dishes with unknown ingredients.

Starters
Fruit, fruit juice, tomato juice.
Avoid pâté, cream soup, shellfish cocktail.

Main course
Fish: grilled or poached.
Poultry, roast or grilled meat, cold meat: trim off any obvious fat or skin.
Avoid sauces, stuffings, dumplings, pastry.

Vegetables
All salads, add dressing of oil and vinegar at the table.
Any vegetable prepared without fat of sauce.
Jacket or boiled potatoes.
Avoid salads already mixed together with rich creamy dressings.
Creamed, roast of fried vegetables.

Bread
Wholemeal bread or rolls, crispbreads.
Avoid butter.

Dessert
Fresh or canned fruit, jelly, sorbet.
Avoid cream, rich creamy ice creams.

To drink
Fruit juice, mineral water, wine, beer and spirits (if permitted).
Coffee, tea.
Avoid cream in coffee or tea.

Remember   If it is impossible to avoid some unsuitable food – have a small helping and satisfy appetite with generous helpings of other foods. The occasional *small* lapse will not cause harm, but it is important to return immediately to your recommended dietary routine.

PACKED SNACKS

Soups
Main course or light soups (see pages 31–35) carried in a thermos flask on cold days.

Wholemeal rolls or sandwiches (in plastic snap bags)
Spread sparingly with polyunsaturated margarine, low-fat margarine spreads or low-calorie salad dressings. Alternatively, leave the bread unspread but make the filling very moist and tasty.

Fillings
Slices of poultry, lean meat or ham – or mince these and mix with chutney, pickles or low-fat sauce.
Canned fish mixed with vinegar, salad dressing (see page 100), tomato purée or bottled sauce.
Cottage or low-fat curd cheese mixed with herbs, sauce, pickles, chopped salad vegetables or chopped grapes.
Home-made pâté (see page 103) spread directly on to bread.
For special occasions, smoked salmon with a squeeze of lemon juice.

To the above fillings, add sliced or shredded salad ingredients and homemade salad dressings.

In cartons
Salads of vegetables, brown rice and pasta mixed with chopped poultry, lean ham or fish and permitted salad dressings.
Accompaniments   Wholemeal bread or rolls, crispbreads, oatcakes.

'Afters'
Fresh or dried fruit and nuts.
Cold desserts in seal-top containers.
Biscuits etc (see Baking section pages 93–100).

To drink
Cold drinks in seal-top tumblers. Coffee or tea with skimmed milk.
Sometimes: canned beer, bottles, cans or cartons of wine or non-alcoholic wine.

CATERING FOR BUFFET MEALS

Select from the following foods:

Starters
Melon, grapefruit, fruit juice.
Home-made pâtés (see pages 103–4) with wholemeal melba toast.
Mixed vegetable broth with added wholemeal cereals, pulse soups, chowders, consommés (see pages 31–33).
Accompaniment to soups   Croutons of wholemeal bread, toasted or fried in polyunsaturated oil.

Main courses
Moderate amounts of fish, meat and cheese (see table on page 22) extended by combining with wholemeal cereals and vegetables, and presented to make a variety of dishes. For example: flans, pizzas, risottos, pasta with succulent meat or fish sauces, casseroles with pulses and other vegetables (see pages 41–43), salmon (or other fish) mousse (see page 77).

Vegetables
Colourful salads made from summer and winter vegetables combined with pulses, brown rice and pastas (see pages 36–40)
Crisply cooked vegetables or vegetable dishes (see pages 41–43).
Potatoes baked or boiled in skins.

Dressings
Home-made French or yoghurt dressings (see pages 100–1).
Proprietary low-calorie dressings
(For use with jacket potatoes as well as salads).

Breads
Wholemeal wheat bread, rye bread and rolls, crispbreads, oatcakes.

Spreads
Tubs of polyunsaturated margarine, low-fat margarine spread and home-made, low-calorie spreads (see page 105).
Some polyunsaturated margarines and spreads may be made into 'pats' using a butter curler.

Desserts
Fresh fruit.
Fresh fruit made up into fruit salads, jellies, cheesecakes and flans
(see pages 88–93).
Fruity puddings such as charlottes and pies.

Accompaniments to dessert   Sorbets, home-made ice cream,
cream substitutes (see pages 91–2).

INDEX

Page numbers in *italics* refer to the illustrations

alcohol, 20
angina, 14, 15
apple: chicken and ham salad with, 36
    low-calorie spread, 105
apricot: apricot whip, 88; *86*
    Turkish orange dessert with, 90
atherosclerosis, 14, 15, 16

baking, 93–100; *95*
banana: banana yoghurt, 89
    Caribbean rumba, 88
barbecue sauce, 102
bean pie, 58
beans in tomato sauce, 107–8
beef: beef and bean goulash, 72–5
    beef and black bean casserole, 70–1
    spaghetti with meat balls, 105–6
    wholemeal spaghetti in sauce, 107
birthday cheesecake, 87–8; *84*
biscuits, 98–9
black beans: beef and black bean casserole, 70–1
    Havana rice and black beans, 110
blackberry: sauce for ice cream, 103
blackcurrant cheesecake, 89–90
blood: cholesterol levels, 11, 13, 14, 16, 21; clots, 20–1
bread, 93–7; *95*

cabbage and raisin salad, 38–9
cake, date and rhubarb, 99; *95*
cancer, 10, 18
Caribbean chicken, 79–80; *83*
Caribbean rumba, 88
cereals, 22
cheese, 25–6
    macaroni in curd cheese sauce, 105
cheesecake, 87–8, 89–90; *84*
chick pea and leek quiche, 57–8

chicken: baked chicken and orange, 80
    Caribbean chicken, 79–80; *83*
    casserole, 68
    chicken à la king, 109
    chicken and rice salad, 36–7; *34*
    chicken, ham and apple salad, 36
    cock-a-leekie soup, 76–7
    curry, 67–8
    lasagne, 48–9
    Moroccan chicken, 68–9
    pâté with walnuts, 77; *84*
    quick chicken charlotte, 67; *62*
    spaghetti with, 106
chilli con carne, 55
cholesterol, 10, 11, 13–14
cock-a-leekie soup, 76–7
coffee ice cream, 91
constipation, 17–18
coronary heart disease, 9–10, 13–17; *9, 15*
cottage pie, 71
country vegetable risotto, 46–7
cracked wheat salad, 40
cream, substitutes, 92–3
Creole baked fish, 79
curry: chicken, 67–8
    dressing, 100–1

dairy products, 23
dates: date and rhubarb cake, 99
    date scones, 97
desserts, 88–93; *84, 86*
diabetes, 10, 16, 18, 20
dieters' ratatouille, 42
dressings, 100–1
drinks, 24
drugs, to reduce cholesterol, 21
Dutch hot-pot, 50–3

eggs, 23
eicosapentaenoic acid, 20–1

fats, in diet, 10–14, 23; *12*
fatty acids, 10, 12, 13, 18
fibre, dietary, 17–20
fish, 22, 60–7, 77–9; *61*
fish pie, 65–6
flans: chick pea and leek, 57–8
  flan cases, 99–100
  red bean flan, 53–4; *52*
French dressing, 101
French onion bread, 94
fromage blanc and fruit, 90–1
fruit, 22, 26
fruit salad, fresh, 87
fruit scones, 97

gallstones, 21
gazpacho, 76
green dressing, 101

haddock: smoked fish lasagne, 48
ham, chicken and apple salad, 36
haricot beans: bean pie, 58
  in green dressing, 38
  Tuscan beans with pasta, 53
  vegetable casserole with, 57
Havana rice and black beans, 110
heart attacks, 9, 11, 13, 14, 15
heart disease, 13, 14–17
high density lipoprotein (HDL),
    13–14, 16, 20
hot-pot with mixed vegetables, 72
hypercholesterolaemia, 10, 13, 21

ice cream, 91
Indonesian rice, 45
intermittent claudication, 15
Italian vegetable soup, 32; *33*

kidney beans: beef goulash, 72–5
  Caribbean chicken, 79–80
  chilli con carne, 55
  Dutch hot-pot, 50–3
  kidney bean risotto, 47
  red bean flan, 53–4; *52*
  red bean pâté, 103–4
  vegetarian bean paella, 56–7

lamb, ragoût of, 75
lasagne, 48–9
lemon sorbet, 92; *86*
lentils: lentil and garlic salad, 37–8
  lentil and split pea loaf, 54; *51*
  lentil bake, 54–5, 81–2; *84*
  Megadarra, 59; *52*

mushroom and lentil pâté, 104
  Scottish lentil broth, 35; *33*
liver: low-calorie liver pâté, 103
low-calorie spread, 105

macaroni in curd cheese sauce, 105
mackerel: croquettes, 66–7
  mousse, 66; *64*
  smoked mackerel pâté, 104
meal plans, 112–21
meat, 20, 23, 26, 69–75; *62, 84*
Megadarra, 59; *52*
Mexican beans, hot, 58–9
milk, 21, 25
monounsaturated fats, 12, 14
Moroccan chicken, 68–9
mousses, savoury, 66, 77–8; *64, 74*
muesli, Oxford, 110–11; *96*
mushroom: pâté with lentils, 104
  mushroom soup, 75–6
  spaghetti with chicken and, 106
  veal escalopes with, 81

Niçoise, salad, 37; *34*
Norwegian bread, 94–7; *95*
nuts, 22
nutty oatmeal biscuits, 99

oats: nutty oatmeal biscuits, 99
  oat popovers, 98
okra Olympia, 43
onion: potatoes with onion, 43
  soup, 31
orange: orange yoghurt juice, 111
  sorbet, 92; *86*
  Turkish apricot dessert with, 90
Oxford muesli, 110–11; *96*

pancakes, 89; *86*
pasta, 30, 32, 47–50, 53
pâtés, 77, 103–4; *84*
peach Cardinal, 82–7
peas, pasta rollers with, 47–8
peas, dried: lentil and split pea
    loaf, 54
  pease pudding, 56
  Scandinavian pea soup, 35; *33*
pheasant in cider, 81–2; *84*
pineapple: Caribbean rumba, 88
piquant dressing, 101
pizza: pizza baps, 109
  quick pizza, 109–10; *96*
plaice piquant, 78–9

polyunsaturated fats, 11–12, 13, 16, 20–1, 26
pork: sweet and sour pork salad, 37
potato: bean pie, 58
  cottage pie, 71
  fish pie, 65–6
  potato salad, 40
  potatoes with onion, 43
poultry, 67–9
protein, 17, 18
pulses, 19–20, 27, 28–9, 50–9; *52*

raspberry: fromage blanc and, 90–1
ratatouille, 42, 50
red cabbage: rotkohl, 42–3
  salad with chestnuts, 39; *34*
rhubarb and date cake, 99
rice, 29–30
  brown rice with orange, 44
  chicken and rice salad, 36–7; *34*
  country vegetable risotto, 46–7
  Havana rice and black beans, 110
  Indonesian rice, 45
  kidney bean risotto, 47
  parsley rice, 46; *62*
  salmon kedgeree, 65
  spicy pilau, 44
  sweetcorn and pepper salad, 39; *64*
  Turkish pilaff, 45
  vegetarian bean paella, 56–7
rissoles, 71; *62*
rotkohl, 42–3
Russian salad, 40

salads, 36–40; *34, 64*
salmon: kedgeree, 65
  mousse with cucumber, 77–8; *74*
sandwiches, toasted turkey, 108; *96*
saturated fats, 11, 13
sauces, 101–3
Scandinavian pea soup, 35; *33*
scones, 97
Scottish lentil broth, 35; *33*
sea bass, Dugléré style, 78

snacks, 103–11
sorbets, 92; *86*
soups, 24, 27, 31–5, 75–7; *33*
soya beans: in tomato sauce, 107–8
  spiced soya toast topper, 108
spaghetti, 105–7
Spanish baked fish, 60
spinach with paprika, 41
strawberries in champagne, 82; *84*
strokes, 15
sugar, 24, 26
summer vegetable casserole, 41
sweet and sour pork salad, 37
sweet and sour veal, 69–70; *62*
sweetcorn, rice and pepper salad, 39; *64*

tomato: gazpacho, 76
  sauce, 101–2, 105–6, 107–8
  tomatoes Provençal, 42; *51*
triglycerides, 11, 16, 20
tuna: pasta with piquant sauce, 49–50
  salade Niçoise, 37; *34*
turkey: toasted sandwiches, 108; *96*
  rice salad with grapes and, 36–7; *34*
Turkish apricot and orange dessert, 90
Turkish pilaff, 45
Tuscan beans with pasta, 53

veal: escalopes with mushrooms, 81
  goulash, 69
  sweet and sour, 69–70; *62*
vegetables, 22, 26, 27, 41–3
vegetarian bean paella, 56–7
vitamins, 10, 18

wholesome fingers, 98

yoghurt, 26
  banana yoghurt, 89
  basic yoghurt dressing, 100
  orange yoghurt juice, 111

Other books in the
Positive Health Guide Series

BEAT HEART DISEASE!
A cardiologist explains how you can help your heart and enjoy a healthier life
Prof Ristéard Mulcahy

HIGH BLOOD PRESSURE
What it means for you, and how to control it
Dr Eoin O'Brien and Prof Kevin O'Malley

THE DIABETICS' DIET BOOK
A new high-fibre eating programme
Dr Jim Mann and the Oxford Dietetic Group

THE DIABETICS' COOKBOOK
Delicious new recipes for entertaining and all the family
Roberta Longstaff, SRD, and Dr Jim Mann

DIABETES
A practical new guide to healthy living
Dr Jim Anderson

THE HIGH-FIBRE COOKBOOK
Recipes for Good Health
Pamela Westland
Introduction by Dr Denis Burkitt

DON'T FORGET FIBRE IN YOUR DIET
To help avoid many of our commonest diseases
Dr Denis Burkitt

THE SALT-FREE DIET BOOK
An appetizing way to help reduce high blood pressure
Dr Graham MacGregor

CHILDREN'S PROBLEMS
A parents' guide to understanding and tackling them
Dr Bryan Lask

THE HYPERACTIVE CHILD
A parents' guide
Dr Eric Taylor

CONTACT LENSES
A guide to successful wear and care
Professor Hikaru Hamano and Professor Montague Ruben